THE Tortoise WORKBOOK

THE Tortoise WORKBOOK

Strategies *for*
Getting Ahead
at Your Own Pace

Sharon Good

New York

© 2003, 2010 Sharon Good

All rights reserved in all media. This book, or parts thereof, may not be reproduced in any form without the express written permission of the author.

Published by:
Good Life Press
A division of Good Life Coaching Inc.

www.goodlifepress.com
www.goodlifecoaching.com
www.beingatortoise.com

Disclaimer: The suggestions in this book are not meant to substitute for professional medical care. If you have or think you have a medical or mental health condition, consult an appropriate professional practitioner.

Library of Congress Control Number: 2010904227

Paperback:
ISBN-13: 978-0-9823172-2-8
ISBN-10: 0-9823172-2-0

E-book:
ISBN-13: 978-0-9823172-3-5
ISBN-10: 0-9823172-3-9

Printed in the United States of America

Contents

The Hare and the Tortoise	1
Welcome and Introduction	2
What's a Tortoise?	3
You're Okay!	4
My Story	5
I've Gotta Be Me	6
Tortoise Issues	7
❧ Energy	7
❧ Time	7
❧ Multiple Focuses and Interests	7
❧ Personal Rhythm	7
❧ The Highly Sensitive Person	7
❧ Emotional Issues	8
❧ Physical Limitations	8
❧ Getting Older	8
❧ Procrastination	9
Tortoises Heroes	11
The Strategies	14
1. Changing Behaviors and Habits	14
2. Calm Down and Slow Down	15
3. Establish Good Boundaries	17
4. Define Success for Yourself	19
5. Manage Goal Setting	22
6. Plan Ahead	25
7. Have Realistic Expectations	27
8. Modify and Compromise	30
9. Keep Your Fears in Check	33
10. Develop Personalized Work Patterns	35
11. Develop Positive Discipline	39
12. Take Care of Yourself	41

13.	Take Energy Breaks	44
14.	Get Help	47
15.	Manage Your Time	49
16.	Set Up Systems	52
17.	Do Short- and Long-Term Planning	54
18.	Break Your Goals Into Steps	56
19.	Know Your Priorities	58
20.	Deal Effectively with Transitions	64
21.	Eliminate Distractions and Learn to Focus	67
22.	Eliminate Energy Drains	70
23.	Enhance the Energy You Have	73
24.	Manage Your Emotions	76
25.	Accept Yourself for Who You Are	82
26.	Reframe Your View	84
27.	Take the Time to Go Deeper	87
28.	Use the Principles of Attraction	89
29.	Stay in the Present Moment	92
30.	Trust the Process	93
31.	Learn Patience and Persistence	94

The Tortoise View	96
Resources	98
Index of Worksheets	101
About the Author	102

The Hare and the Tortoise

by Aesop

A Hare one day ridiculed the short feet and slow pace of the Tortoise, who replied, laughing: "Though you be swift as the wind, I will beat you in a race." The Hare, believing her assertion to be simply impossible, assented to the proposal; and they agreed that the Fox should choose the course and fix the goal.

On the day appointed for the race, the two started together. The Tortoise never for a moment stopped, but went on with a slow but steady pace straight to the end of the course. The Hare, lying down by the wayside, fell fast asleep. At last waking up, and moving as fast as he could, he saw the Tortoise had reached the goal, and was comfortably dozing after her fatigue.

Slow but steady wins the race.

Translated by George Fyler Townsend

Welcome and Introduction

Welcome to *The Tortoise Workbook*!

This book will offer you comfort in being who you are as well as ideas and strategies to help you maximize your available resources. As a Tortoise myself, I've spent years honing my coping strategies. And while we're all works in progress and there's always more to learn and develop, I've come a long way in being able to carry through with my projects without exhausting myself. I hope to share some of what I've learned with you.

I suggest that you read this book through once to pick up the major ideas, and then refer back to specific sections and worksheets as needed. Use the worksheets to get a deeper understanding of the ideas and strategies, and redo appropriate ones from time to time as you develop proficiency in using the tools and techniques in the book.

Whether you define yourself as a Tortoise or not, I invite you to use the information and exercises in this book to streamline your life and become more efficient and productive at whatever you do.

Sharon Good

> *"Confidence, like art, never comes from having all the answers;*
> *it comes from being open to all the questions."*
> — Earl Gray Stevens

What's a "Tortoise"?

I define a Tortoise as someone with lots of ideas and ambition, but limited energy, time or other resources. You may become easily frustrated or discouraged when the ideas, opportunities and projects come along faster than you can handle them. Like the Tortoise in the fable, we human Tortoises need to go slowly and take a step at a time. It's important for us to have strategies to help us make the most of our time and energy.

There's a range of people that fall under this Tortoise definition, including:

- Those with low energy, either because that's their natural rhythm or because of a medical cause, such as chronic fatigue, hypothyroid, bipolar disorder or any injury, illness or condition that slows you down
- Those who are very busy or don't have enough time to do everything they want, including working or single parents or those with many interests and focuses
- Some creative or "right-brain" types who generate ideas at a faster pace than they can execute them
- Those who like to do things slowly or have a slower personal rhythm or cadence
- Those who like to think things through and make decisions slowly, or who have difficulty making choices
- Those who need to have a solid understanding of what they're doing before they feel comfortable doing it
- Those who can only process a certain amount of information input at a time
- Those who get derailed by strong emotions and have difficulty functioning
- Those who don't feel they're working up to their potential
- Those who are easily distracted and find it hard to focus
- The Highly Sensitive Person (HSP), as defined by Elaine Aron in her book of that name, who is easily overwhelmed by life and needs a lot of recovery time

You may exhibit one or more of these "conditions" or some other reason that keeps you from accomplishing as much as you'd like. Whatever the reason, it can be frustrating and rob you of self-confidence. But Tortoise or not, each of us has our strengths and limitations, and the strategies in this book will help you to maximize your strengths and work with your limitations.

> *"Whether we like it or not, each of us is constrained by limits on what we can do and feel. To ignore these limits leads to denial and eventually to failure. To achieve excellence, we must first understand the reality of the everyday, with all its demands and potential frustrations."*
> — Mihaly Csikszentmihalyi, *Finding Flow: The Psychology of Engagement With Everyday Life*

You're Okay!

Being a Tortoise is okay! We live in a world that values speed and accomplishment, but many older traditions value being in the moment and exploring the depth of whatever we're focusing on. In Buddhism, for example, we find the concept of "mindfulness" — paying full attention to what you're doing, rather than rushing through or multitasking.

Being a Tortoise is not just about keeping up with others; it can be about keeping up with all that *you* want to accomplish. For any creative person, it's a lot easier to come up with ideas than to implement them. If you're also time- or energy-challenged, it can be that much more frustrating trying to juggle all you want to do.

In his book, *Timeshifting*, Stephan Rechtschaffen talks about how children are taught that life is a race. There's a performance expectation from our parents and teachers. We're given timed tests and assume that if we can come up with the answers fast, we're smart, and if we can't, we're not. Rechtschaffen says, "Brilliance is about creativity and depth of understanding, not about the speed of performance."

For some of us, trying to keep up with our friends and colleagues becomes painful. We force ourselves to do things faster than is comfortable, and perhaps sacrifice quality in the process, or we push ourselves to endure more than we're capable of, sometimes jeopardizing our health or well-being. You might party all night or participate in sports, only to end up in bed recovering for the next couple of days. And to add insult to injury, the party or the sports may not even be fun for you.

In her book, *Live the Life You Love*, Barbara Sher says, "Our culture often equates the ability to endure punishment with excellence. . . . A lot of people with other kinds of genius get thrown on the trash heap when endurance is the main measure of worthiness. I wonder how many gifted people are walking around thinking they don't have what it takes because they couldn't make it through gym class, or a punishing college experience, or some other endurance-based change model."

We need to discover our own unique strengths and gifts, even though they may not be the more highly-prized ones in our social group. We can give them value ourselves and find people who appreciate them. We can define our lives based on what serves us and makes us happy.

Being a Tortoise doesn't mean you have to give up your dreams, but you do need to learn to work with your limitations. You can modify your dreams so that they're reachable for you and use the techniques in this book to accomplish them. And that's a lot more fun than setting yourself up with unattainable goals and a lifetime of disappointment and frustration.

Learning to accept ourselves is a challenge each one of us faces. If we're outside the norm of our social group, it's that much harder. Self-acceptance is crucial, and we need to build our self-esteem to the point where we can find value in ourselves despite the messages we're getting from those around us, or we need to find new communities that accept and enjoy us for who we are.

> *"Keep away from people who try to belittle your ambitions. Small people always do that, but the really great make you feel that you, too, can become great."*
> — Mark Twain

My Story

I'm a person with lots of ideas and ambition, but, unfortunately, a low supply of energy. The ideas come fast and furious, but if I push myself as fast as I'd like to go, I'm knocked out by mid-afternoon. I have a lot of ideas I want to get out to the world, through writing and teaching, and projects I want to accomplish. My to-do list is pretty daunting. (A friend of mine gasped when she saw it.)

In 1990, I cofounded a small publishing company, Excalibur Publishing. It was exciting, but also scary to have that much responsibility and deal with risking larger sums of money than I ever had before. Out of fear, I forced myself to work on it whenever I was not at my three-day "survival" job. I developed what became my typical "downward spiral" pattern: I would push myself to the limit, until my nerves were jangled. Then, I would either sleep badly or not enough. When I woke up tired, nerves still frazzled, I would feel anxious and overwhelmed, and my thoughts would take a negative turn, imagining all the worst things that could happen. I would then be fearful, pressured and angry. Not a powerful way to operate.

We managed to publish fourteen books in seven years, but I was constantly scared and stressed and ended up in major burn-out. My partner and I decided, at that point, not to publish any new titles. Being downsized from my day job a few months later gave me six much-needed months to recover.

At the same time, I was approaching middle age, and I attributed my decreased energy to getting older and hormonal changes. I felt there was nothing I could do about it but accept it and work with it. On the positive side, it forced me to learn more efficient ways of conducting myself, so that I could accomplish more with less energy. I discovered that worry was a huge energy drain and time waster for me. The more I could release it, the more I got done, with less effort. And a few years down the road, I was fortunate to discover that some of my energy loss was due to hypothyroid, which is treatable, and my energy level improved with medication.

When I became a Life Coach, I vowed to do things differently and not run myself into the ground. In the beginning it was easy, as I was patient with myself while I learned and explored my new field. But as time passed, I felt that my colleagues expected more of me. (In truth, I was the one expecting more of myself.) As I watched some of them run circles around me with their accomplishments and achievements, I felt I needed to push myself harder. But it didn't work; I just burned myself out more.

As I mulled over this dilemma, it occurred to me that even if I could push myself harder, I would hate it. I didn't want to create a life where I dreaded getting up every day. I needed to accept my limitations and maximize my strengths, and I needed a way to reframe my experience to make it positive.

What came to me was the fable of "The Hare and the Tortoise." The image of the slow, steady Tortoise suited me perfectly. I could certainly take small, slow, persistent steps and accomplish the things I wanted. Whenever I felt upset at not being able to do all I hoped to do, I would simply remind myself that I was a Tortoise, and my pace was "slow and steady." That would calm me down and keep me going. And I didn't let myself forget that the Tortoise won the race!

By functioning well as a Tortoise, I've been able to accomplish a lot and to enjoy the process. There are times when I forget and start to drive myself again, but it becomes easier to remember. I focus on what I can do rather than what I can't. I can now hold my head high, appreciating my accomplishments and the effort behind them.

I've Gotta Be Me

Being a Tortoise doesn't mean having to twist yourself into a pretzel to conform to other people's ideas of how things should be done. We need to find our own identity and feel good about it. And while we all need to conform to *some* outside standards, we need to look inside to define ourselves on a deeper level.

We all do our best when we're authentic about who we are. When you try to deny it and work against it, it's like swimming upstream. It takes ten times the energy to get something done than if you did it in a way that's natural to you. It takes energy to pretend to be something you're not, and that energy could be used more productively to accomplish the things that are meaningful to you.

The word "integrity" comes from the root word "integer," which means something that's whole or complete. When we honor who we are, we live in integrity. There's a sense of alignment between who we are and what we do. This is true for everyone, and for us Tortoises, it's particularly important, not just for our productivity, but for our self-esteem. If we try to live up to other people's standards, we'll never hit the mark, and we'll suffer in many ways.

So, be proud of who you are and honor it in your choices and actions. Remember, it's not just the gifts you were endowed with, but how you use them that counts. All you can do is to do your best.

> *"The key to the ability to change is a changeless sense of who you are, what you are about and what you value."*
> — Stephen Covey, *The 7 Habits of Highly Effective People*

Tortoise Issues

Like any other "syndrome," being a Tortoise can show up in a number of ways. Most likely, you'll relate to one or more of these "symptoms."

Energy

This is the defining issue for many Tortoises, whether we have chronic fatigue, low thyroid or simply naturally low energy. This may not be a problem by itself, except that it can prevent you from doing the things you want to do. You may have to scale down your efforts or eliminate certain projects or activities that are just too taxing for you. If your major challenge is time, lack of sleep or poor self-care may add low energy to your list of issues.

Time

In this busy world, with most of us already multitasking, we never have the time to do everything we want to do. You may be working, in a marriage or relationship, parenting, going to school, or have any other number of responsibilities and obligations. If you have a calling or drive to accomplish something "extra" — write a book or screenplay, become a great golfer, paint, do volunteer work — the time issue is compounded. You may have an adequate supply of energy under "normal" circumstances, but when you try to fit in everything you need and want to do, time becomes scarce.

Multiple Focuses and Interests

Some of us have a myriad of interests that we try to cram into one life. We never seem to have the time or energy to do it all, and we feel frustrated. This is a common complaint with many creative types. (Being creative is not limited to artists.) Prioritizing and short- and long-term planning are particularly important for managing this issue. For the specific challenges of attention deficit disorder (ADD), there are books available with techniques to help you focus.

Personal Rhythm

Some people are slow movers by nature. You may need a period of contemplation before a period of action. You may need to understand something deeply before you act on it. Or you may like to explore on a deeper level, valuing the learning more than the accomplishment. When you try to override this pattern, you feel scattered or off-balance and don't derive the satisfaction you crave from these activities.

The Highly Sensitive Person

The Highly Sensitive Person (HSP) is a designation created by Elaine Aron in her popular books. Some doctors are even using it as a diagnosis! An HSP is someone whose nervous system is more sensitive and more easily overstimulated than the average person's. Aron claims that about 20 percent of the population tends to be highly sensitive.

HSPs often have difficulty with intense physical stimulation, such as noise and bright lights, as well as emotional stimulation. Social interaction or any intense effort, even when enjoyable, can be draining. After a social encounter, HSPs often need to sequester themselves for awhile to recover. Therefore, they may need to limit certain activities or allot extra time to deal with the after-effects.

Some HSPs may suffer from extreme sensitivities, such as chemical sensitivities, which limit their interaction with a world in which exposure to someone's perfume can cause a migraine headache or intense social interaction can put them in bed for a few days.

Emotional Issues

Some of us have chronic emotional issues that can stop us in our tracks. These include fear, self-doubt, worry, guilt, anxiety and depression, among others. Some of these need to be handled professionally. The garden variety can generally be handled with self-management techniques learned through self-help books and workshops.

In addition, for some of us, when we're dealing with an upsetting situation, we become consumed by it, and it becomes difficult to get anything done. We can't get focused. We may be easily distracted or find it difficult to deal with new situations and challenges. Again, we can develop strategies and techniques to manage these.

Emotional issues may also include emotional scars that we continue to carry with us that make us feel we can't accomplish our goals. Even if you suffered some sort of trauma as a child or adult, it is possible to heal and transcend. Many of our great teachers began by healing themselves and then teaching others how to follow in their footsteps.

Emotional issues are just touched on in this book, as it is a huge area unto itself. If this is an issue for you, there are numerous books, workshops and professional resources to help you work it through and create coping strategies for yourself.

Physical Limitations

There are many physical conditions that can limit how much you can do, including injury and illness. While this can be frustrating, it doesn't have to stop you completely. Your professional medical team can help you with some of those issues, and the strategies in this book will give you additional techniques and tools to work with. There are many great role models to encourage you (see Tortoise Heroes).

Getting Older

Most of us experience a slowing down or other physical changes or limitations as we get older. Along with these physical imperatives, we may simply no longer see the value in achievement for its own sake. It's not uncommon for people to become more inner-directed as they get older. We need time to assimilate and adapt to the physical/mental/emotional changes that come with age, to decide what's really important to us and what we want to devote our time and energy to. We can find ways to work more efficiently and effectively, with depth, rather than doing too much too fast.

Procrastination

Procrastination is often a symptom or function of another issue. For example, in *The Tomorrow Trap*, author Karen E. Peterson, Ph.D. claims that procrastination is a way we protect ourselves from anticipated shame or humiliation if we move forward with the task we're avoiding.

For us Tortoises, procrastination could be a function of feeling overwhelmed, being afraid of becoming frustrated with our slowness or of falling short of our vision. By uncovering the reason(s) you procrastinate, you can make some behavioral modifications to move through it.

Use the following worksheet to make note of the Tortoise Issues you need to address.

Worksheet I: My Tortoise Issues

Check off your Tortoise Issues. Include any personal notes or comments that will help you to better understand how it operates for you.

- ❏ Energy
- ❏ Time
- ❏ Multiple Focuses and Interests
- ❏ Personal Rhythm
- ❏ Highly Sensitive Person
- ❏ Emotional Issues:
  - ❏ Fear
  - ❏ Self-doubt
  - ❏ Worry
  - ❏ Guilt
  - ❏ Anxiety
  - ❏ Depression
  - ❏ Get caught up in the dramas of my life
  - ❏ Past hurts
  - ❏ Other _____
- ❏ Physical Limitations
- ❏ Getting Older
  - ❏ Less energy
  - ❏ Need more sleep
  - ❏ Not as strong
  - ❏ Not motivated to push myself
- ❏ Procrastination

  In what areas do you procrastinate?

  What are you trying to avoid by procrastinating?

Tortoise Heroes

We all need heroes. When we're facing a challenge, it's encouraging to know that there are others who have faced it before us and triumphed. There are numerous Tortoises who succeeded despite their Tortoise Issue. I'm sure you can think of many unsung heroes who have overcome their challenges and succeeded in their own way, on their own terms — maybe even yourself. Here are a few of the "sung" heroes to inspire you. I'm sure you'll begin to notice many more on your own.

- Despite a weak constitution, Jean François Champollion began as a teenager relentlessly pursuing the meaning of the Rosetta Stone. His 1822 paper on deciphering hieroglyphs enabled future Egyptologists to read inscriptions that had been silent for fifteen hundred years. He died at the age of forty-one.

- Actor Christopher Reeve, an avid athlete, suffered a debilitating injury that left him a quadriplegic. Even so, this courageous man continued his acting career, made his directorial debut, wrote two books (***Still Me*** and ***Nothing Is Impossible: Reflections on a New Life***) and was active as a much-sought-after motivational speaker and activist for spinal cord injury research.

- Stricken with chronic fatigue syndrome while in college, and later adding vertigo to her challenges, Laura Hillenbrand's passion for horse racing led her on a journey that began with writing articles for equine magazines and culminated in writing the best-selling book and hit movie, *Seabiscuit*. At one point, it took her six weeks to write a 1500-word article, and writing the book took a toll on her health. She still hopes to write another.

- At the height of his career, actor Michael J. Fox was diagnosed with Parkinson's disease. Nine years later, he semi-retired from acting and founded the Michael J. Fox Foundation, focusing his energies on advocating for research to cure Parkinson's. He has written two books, ***Lucky Man: A Memoir*** and ***Always Looking Up: The Adventures of an Incurable Optimist***, and continues to make occasional TV appearances.

- Stephen Hawking rose to become an acclaimed physicist and author (***A Brief History of Time*** and ***The Universe in a Nutshell***) despite a motor neurone disease that came on when he was studying for his Ph.D. Hawking needs a computer to talk and write, both very slowly. This Brit complained that the computer that he talks with gives him an American accent.

- Athletes Michelle Akers (U.S. Olympic soccer team, gold medalists in Atlanta), Peter Marshall (British World Cup soccer) and Amy Peterson (Olympic gold speed skater) all suffered from CFIDS (chronic fatigue).

- Jackie Joyner-Kersee, "the world's best female athlete," overcame poverty and asthma to become a three-time Olympic gold medalist, world record-holder and motivational speaker.

- Irish painter Christy Brown, born with cerebral palsy, painted with the only limb over which he had control. His story is told in the film, ***My Left Foot***.

- Theologian/writer/speaker Irene Monroe was abandoned by her mother at age six months. She was placed with a foster mother who constantly told her, "You come from nothing, you are nothing, you'll be nothing." At the age of six or seven, she realized that she had an inner strength and that the world was open to her like everybody else. Seeing that education was her ticket out, she worked hard and created opportunities to pursue higher education at Wellesley, Columbia and Harvard.

- Thomas Alva Edison, one of our greatest inventors, did not learn to talk until he was almost four years old. He was a difficult student who would probably be diagnosed today with Attention Deficit Disorder. His mother home-schooled him. Severe hearing loss prevented him from pursuing higher education, but he taught himself science through reading and experimentation. He filed 1,093 successful U.S. patents, including the light bulb, the phonograph and the first talking moving pictures, as well as more than five hundred unsuccessful ones.

- Ayn Rand took twelve years to write *Atlas Shrugged*.

- Napoleon Hill was encouraged in 1908 by Dale Carnegie to organize the world's first philosophy of personal achievement. He developed the material over several decades. *Think and Grow Rich*, published in 1937, is still the all-time best-seller in motivational books.

Who are your Tortoise heroes? Use the following worksheet to list them.

> "The world is moved not only by the mighty shoves of the heroes, but also by the aggregate of the tiny pushes of each honest worker."
> — Helen Keller

Worksheet 2: My Tortoise Heroes

List some of your Tortoise heroes and what you admire about them, how they inspire you.

Who: _____

Why:_____

_____

_____

Who: _____

Why:_____

_____

_____

Who: _____

Why:_____

_____

_____

Who: _____

Why:_____

_____

_____

Who: _____

Why:_____

_____

_____

The Strategies

Just about anything can be handled when you have a plan. Once you know what your Tortoise Issues are, you can develop strategies for dealing with them effectively. Here are a few ways to make your Tortoise-ness work for you. They're not presented in any particular order. Pick out the ones that work for you, and feel free to come up with more of your own. Use the worksheets to get more clarity on how these strategies can work best for you, and rework them from time to time as you refine the process.

1. Changing Behaviors and Habits

Before we jump in, I want to say a few words on this subject. A lot of us hold the myth that we're supposed to be able to change long-held behaviors either instantly or not at all. Think of the smoker who's trying to quit or the dieter trying to lose weight. We may feel inspired in the beginning and pull it off effortlessly, only to revert to our old habits after a week or two.

Keep in mind that some of the strategies in this book will be a radical departure from your current habits, and it may take time and continual reinforcement to keep them in place. It will be tempting to get discouraged and quit if they don't work right away.

The truth is, most often, changing a behavior takes repetition, practice and renewal. By renewal, I mean that if you revert to your old habit, rather than quitting in despair, thinking it's hopeless, start again. And again and again and again if necessary. Each time you start over, it will get a little easier, until somewhere down the line, the new habit will be firmly in place. And even then, if the old habit creeps back in, renew your efforts once again.

Don't beat yourself up for not getting it right on the first try. Punishing or berating yourself is not going to make it happen any faster. If anything, use a positive reward system to motivate yourself to stay with it, and celebrate even minor successes.

Be aware also that it's not going to be a straight run. You may get on a great schedule, only to have an emergency or a vacation turn it upside down for a week or two. Renew. Your energy may fluctuate from week to week. Work with what you've got and continually renew your efforts. Hold tenaciously to your intention to put your new habits in place, and in good time, they'll become part of your daily routine.

> *"Be patient with yourself. Self-growth is tender; it's holy ground. There's no greater investment."*
> — Stephen Covey, *The 7 Habits of Highly Effective People*

2. Calm Down and Slow Down

As Tortoises, when we feel we're not accomplishing enough, we tend to get panicky and drive ourselves harder. Not good. In the long run, we will accomplish more by honoring our natural rhythms and ways of working. The goal is to "work smarter, not harder," and many of the strategies in this book will help you do that.

Keep in mind that it's important to have depth to what you do, not just speed. Life is more satisfying when you enjoy the journey and learn from it, rather than just running from goal to goal. In *The Power of Full Engagement*, authors Jim Loehr and Tony Schwartz assert that one of the ways we drain our energy is by multitasking. Take the time to do one thing with full attention before you move onto the next. Strive to perform with excellence rather than speed, with quality rather than quantity.

Set the pace for your day by starting from a calm place. If necessary, get up fifteen to thirty minutes before the other members of the household. Use whatever methods work for you: reading, music, meditation, prayer, doing yoga or tai chi, sitting in silence, doing knitting or needlepoint, taking a walk in nature, looking at beautiful pictures, taking in an aromatherapy scent, whatever. Create your own ritual. For some people, quietly reading the newspaper gets the day off to a good start; for others, it's important to avoid the overstimulation of TV or news. Discover what works best for you.

Use these same methods at the end of the day to end it calmly and quietly, so that you can get a full, peaceful night's sleep and begin the next day fully rested.

> *"If you're having difficulty coming up with new ideas, then slow down. For me, slowing down has been a tremendous source of creativity. It has allowed me to open up – to know that there's life under the earth and that I have to let it come through me in a new way. Creativity exists in the present moment. You can't find it anywhere else."*
> — Natalie Goldberg

Worksheet 3: Morning and Evening Rituals

My Morning Ritual

- ❏ Listen to soft music
- ❏ Read something inspirational
- ❏ Read something relaxing
- ❏ Take a walk in nature
- ❏ Meditate
- ❏ Take a long shower
- ❏ Take a hot bath
- ❏ Say prayers
- ❏ Read scripture
- ❏ Sit quietly
- ❏ Do yoga / tai chi / chi gong
- ❏ Do knitting, crocheting or needlepoint
- ❏ Review the day to come
- ❏ Talk with someone
- ❏ Light a candle or burn incense
- ❏ Breathe deeply
- ❏ Do light exercise or stretching
- ❏ Look out the window
- ❏ Have a hot drink (noncaffeinated)
- ❏ _____
- ❏ _____
- ❏ _____
- ❏ _____
- ❏ _____
- ❏ _____
- ❏ _____
- ❏ _____
- ❏ _____
- ❏ _____
- ❏ _____
- ❏ _____

My Evening Ritual

- ❏ Listen to soft music
- ❏ Read something inspirational
- ❏ Read something relaxing
- ❏ Take a walk in nature
- ❏ Meditate
- ❏ Take a long shower
- ❏ Take a hot bath
- ❏ Say prayers
- ❏ Read scripture
- ❏ Sit quietly
- ❏ Do yoga / tai chi / chi gong
- ❏ Do knitting, crocheting or needlepoint
- ❏ Review the day past
- ❏ Talk with someone
- ❏ Light a candle or burn incense
- ❏ Breathe deeply
- ❏ Do light exercise or stretching
- ❏ Look out the window
- ❏ Have a hot drink (noncaffeinated)
- ❏ _____
- ❏ _____
- ❏ _____
- ❏ _____
- ❏ _____
- ❏ _____
- ❏ _____
- ❏ _____
- ❏ _____
- ❏ _____
- ❏ _____
- ❏ _____

3. Establish Good Boundaries

There are times when you're going to need to protect yourself from outside influences by setting boundaries. Think of boundaries as your "tortoise shell," your way to protect your sensitive and vulnerable areas. If you're Highly Sensitive, this will be particularly important in order for you to conserve your energy and stay focused.

Some ways to do this:

- Say "no" when you feel overextended. If this is difficult for you, write a script and practice or role-play it until it becomes easier. A "no" stated as a simple response, without anger or attitude, will be better received than defensiveness or counterattack. There's no need to feel guilty or that you need to explain or justify yourself. Taking care of yourself is justification enough. If you feel angry with someone because they've overstepped your boundaries in the past, let them know, if appropriate, or let your anger out privately, perhaps in a journal, and come to peace with it, so you can respond with a calm "no, thanks" in the future.

- Think of the people you especially need to set boundaries with. It may be a coworker who insists on coming into your office to gab first thing in the morning, when you're barely awake, or a friend who phones at inappropriate times. Clearly state the boundary ("I need you not to call before 10 AM"). If they continue to violate it, take an action such as turning off the phone ringer until you're ready to receive calls. If it's someone close to you, explain to them what you're doing, so they don't worry when you don't answer.

- Eliminate distractions, so you can concentrate. Don't feel you need to respond to every ring of the phone or the doorbell. Let voicemail pick up your calls. Don't feel compelled to constantly check e-mail. Close your door and place a "do not disturb" sign when you need to concentrate, or take your laptop to the library or a coffee bar.

- Set aside blocks of time to do your work. Mark this time in your planner and hold it sacred, not to be relinquished to respond to others' needs (unless it's a small child or an emergency, of course). Hold this boundary as inviolable, and teach the people in your life to honor it.

- Stand up for your needs when other people don't understand or honor them. Tortoises will often have greater, or different, needs than their family and coworkers, who might see your needs as excessive or self-indulgent and be intolerant of them. Be patient with them — realize that they just don't understand how you feel — but be firm about taking care of yourself.

- Let it be okay to do things the way you need to, rather than waiting for someone else to give you permission to be who you are. Let people know that, for instance, because you work slower, you're not slacking off. Find an occupation and work environment that suits your tempo. Experiment to find your own best ways of working.

- Remember, too, to recognize and honor the boundaries of other Tortoises, even if they're not aware of them themselves.

"One can have no smaller or greater mastery than mastery of oneself."
— Leonardo da Vinci

Worksheet 4: Setting Boundaries

How I Need to Set Boundaries

- ❏ Say "no" to _____

- ❏ Eliminate distractions:

  _____   _____

  _____   _____

  _____   _____

- ❏ Honor my work time
- ❏ Honor the way I work
- ❏ Honor my physical and emotional needs
- ❏ _____
- ❏ _____
- ❏ _____
- ❏ _____

Who I Need to Set Boundaries With

Name: _____

Boundary I need to set: _____

_____

_____

What I need to communicate (include the exact words to use as a script, if that will be helpful):

_____

_____

_____

_____

4. DEFINE SUCCESS FOR YOURSELF

One of our greatest pitfalls as a Tortoise is trying to keep up with everyone else. We get caught up in the dreams and goals of our colleagues and what is touted as success in our society. We forget to ask ourselves what *we* want and end up running ourselves ragged trying to live out other people's ideas of success.

We need to define success on our own terms. And we need to be realistic about it. That may mean making some compromises. I have colleagues who work twelve hours a day and are exhilarated by it. Not me. Even if I have a good day and manage to do that, I generally pay for it the next day, waking up drained and draggy and not getting much done that day. I need to pace myself, or else plan to sleep in the morning after a whirlwind day. I need to have down time to recuperate and refresh.

Perhaps energy isn't your challenge, but time. You may be a parent holding down a full-time job, trying to do it all. Just doing the things you *have* to do takes up all your time, and you think wistfully of your dreams languishing on the side. You may need to scale down your idea of success or restructure it for the long term, starting small and building momentum as time becomes more available. By defining your most important values, you can use them as a guideline in making choices that are in your best interest, instead of deferring to the values and choices of the people around you or the ones you pick up from the media.

Discover what's really important to you, what your core values are, and then take into account your Tortoise Issues. For example, if making a lot of money is important to you, find a way to do it that includes your Tortoise Issue. Look at the degree. Is it about becoming a multimillionaire or about being able to retire comfortably by age 60? Is it worth pushing yourself to do that, or would you be happier working for more years at an easier pace? If you're seeking recognition, does it have to be *People* magazine recognition, or is the company newsletter or praise from your boss enough? Get to the essence of what you want, and find ways to achieve it that don't push you beyond your capacities.

Reframe success to enjoy what you're doing, rather than focusing only on the end goal. Big wins are great, but the exhilaration passes quickly and you find yourself driven to the next one. If you enjoy the day-to-day of what you do, you're winning every day, without paying for it with your health and well-being.

> *"Success, in my view, is the willingness to strive for something you really want. The person not reaching the top is no less a success than the one who achieved it, if they both sweated blood, sweat and tears and overcame obstacles and fears. The failure to be perfect does not mean you're not a success."*
> — Fran Tarkenton

Worksheet 5: Life / Work Values

What's Important to Me

- ❏ Achievement
- ❏ Recognition
- ❏ Peace
- ❏ Family / friends
- ❏ Prosperity / material things
- ❏ Challenge
- ❏ Comfort
- ❏ Happiness
- ❏ Independence / autonomy
- ❏ Security
- ❏ Good health
- ❏ Integrity
- ❏ Personal fulfillment
- ❏ Self-expression
- ❏ Fun
- ❏ Contributing
- ❏ Creativity
- ❏ Having good quality-of-life
- ❏ Sense of accomplishment
- ❏ Learning / knowledge
- ❏ Feeling valued
- ❏ Using my skills and abilities
- ❏ Prestige / status
- ❏ Creating or building something
- ❏ Personal growth and development
- ❏ Social interaction
- ❏ Physical strength and ability
- ❏ Belonging
- ❏ _____
- ❏ _____
- ❏ _____

- ❏ Adventure
- ❏ Excitement
- ❏ Exploration
- ❏ Beauty
- ❏ Spirituality / religion
- ❏ Teaching / influencing
- ❏ Feeling needed
- ❏ Pursuing my passion(s)
- ❏ Acceptance
- ❏ Taking risks
- ❏ Supporting a social cause
- ❏ Doing meaningful work
- ❏ Feeling useful
- ❏ Helping
- ❏ Looking good
- ❏ Being productive
- ❏ Staying active
- ❏ Variety
- ❏ Stability / consistency
- ❏ Winning / succeeding
- ❏ Being a team player
- ❏ Staying current
- ❏ Enjoying the pleasures of life
- ❏ Leaving a legacy
- ❏ Accumulating wealth
- ❏ Solitude
- ❏ Communicating
- ❏ Mentoring
- ❏ _____
- ❏ _____
- ❏ _____

Worksheet 6: Defining My Success

How do you define success for yourself?

Look at the following areas and write out what success means to you in that area:

- Career
- Money and Finances
- Family
- Friends/Community
- Significant Other/Romance
- Physical Environment
- Fun/Recreation
- Creativity/Self-Expression
- Health/Self-Care
- Personal Growth/Spirituality

Now, look again at each area.

- Is this definition yours, or does it come from someone else?
  If that person were out of the picture, how would you redefine this area?

- Do you see any conflicts among the different areas?
  How could you resolve these conflicts?

- Does your definition of success feel attainable?
  If not, what can you do to modify it so it does?

5. Manage Goal Setting

Setting goals can be a valuable tool when it's done with your well-being in mind — which should be your first goal! Often, we take on too many goals or underestimate how long it will take to complete them. Then, we make ourselves crazy or sick trying to get it all done.

Begin by being selective about which goals you choose. Don't take on more than you can handle. Choose goals that feel doable for you, and set your own pace and time frame. Break your big goals down into small steps and prioritize them. Put them on a time line or in your planner. (See sections 17 [Do Short- and Long-Term Planning], 18 [Break Your Goals Into Steps] and 19 [Know Your Priorities].)

If you're motivated by deadlines, by all means set them, but be flexible with them in case you've underestimated how much time you'll need or if other parts of your life intrude. Plan ahead, and give yourself lots of lead time to accomplish a goal. Have backup plans in case things go awry.

If you have a tendency to procrastinate and leave things till the last minute, start to develop new habits. Start well in advance, and take steps on a regular basis. Create a schedule and time line that you can stick to, and find someone who will hold you accountable if you drop the ball. Reward yourself when you follow through.

Notice, too, if your goals are your own. It's not uncommon to take on goals that you pick up from other people or the world around you. If your goals are not your own, you'll probably find yourself resisting and procrastinating, which only drains your energy more. If you're doing that, ask yourself, Is this something I truly want to do? If not, cross it off your list, or complete it this time and remember not to take it on again.

Use the following worksheets to list your goals for the specified time periods, and then break each goal into steps. For short-term goals, list the specific tasks you need to do. For longer goals, break it down into the big steps. For example, if you want to make a career change in five years, your goals might include finding a training program or college, going through the application process, starting school, getting your degree and looking for a new job. Then, take the first step (finding a training program or college) and list the specific tasks you need to do for that.

Finally, get yourself a paper or electronic calendar or planner. Enter the immediate tasks you want to accomplish, either on specific dates or on a general to-do list. I particularly like electronic planners, because the to-do list items carry over if they're not accomplished on the assigned date.

As with all the techniques in this book, use goal setting in the way that best serves you to optimize your use of time and energy.

"Once we have identified our special talents, it doesn't matter whether or not we find immediate success in them; what does matter is that we take a step each day towards our intended goal!"
— Josh Hinds

Worksheet 7: My Goals

Things I'd Like to Accomplish in the Next…

Week:

Month:

6 Months:

Year:

5 Years:

10 Years:

20 Years:

Worksheet 8: Breaking Down Goals Into Steps

Goal: _____

Tasks or steps:

1. _____
2. _____
3. _____
4. _____
5. _____
6. _____
7. _____
8. _____
9. _____
10. _____

Goal: _____

Tasks or steps:

1. _____
2. _____
3. _____
4. _____
5. _____
6. _____
7. _____
8. _____
9. _____
10. _____

6. Plan Ahead

Planning ahead is probably the strategy that saves me the most wear and tear. I don't work well under pressure, and hard-and-fast deadlines make me nervous, so whenever possible, I start well in advance and take steps on a regular basis, so that I'm not scrambling to get it all done at the last minute.

When something needs to get done by a certain date and you let it go until the last minute, you can wear yourself down physically and mentally trying to get it all done at once. You may worry or panic. It may keep you awake nights in fear that you won't meet your deadline and be embarrassed or humiliated. You may resort to unhealthy tactics, like staying up all night or guzzling caffeine. You may find yourself in a bad mood, snapping at the people you care about. You suffer and your other concerns suffer.

When you have a project with a deadline, work back from your deadline, and figure out how much time you'll need to complete the tasks involved. Start early, and do a little bit at a time, so that you can easily finish on time. Use the tips in sections 5 (Manage Goal Setting) and 18 (Break Your Goals Into Steps) to break down the project and plan your work flow in a timely way.

Planning ahead, so that you can work without pressure, makes it easier on your nervous system and makes the project less daunting. And the added bonus: You might actually enjoy it more!

"A stitch in time saves nine."
— Traditional Proverb

Worksheet 9: Project Planning

Project name: _____

Deadline date: _____

List the steps you need to take to complete this project, in chronological order. Assign completion dates to each step, working back from the deadline date.

Step	Complete by
_____	_____
_____	_____
_____	_____
_____	_____
_____	_____
_____	_____
_____	_____
_____	_____
_____	_____
_____	_____
_____	_____
_____	_____
_____	_____
_____	_____
_____	_____
_____	_____
_____	_____
_____	_____
_____	_____

7. Have Realistic Expectations

Part of my definition of Tortoises is that we have dreams, goals and ambitions. We may even be driven to achieve. But our Tortoise Issue keeps us from moving as fast as we'd like. Often, we can come up with ideas a lot faster than we can implement them. Or we have grand dreams, but not the resources to achieve them.

In order to avoid frustrating and discouraging ourselves, we need to have realistic expectations about what we can accomplish. Having huge goals that you can't achieve sets you up for failure. By setting realistic goals and taking small steps, you set yourself up to succeed, which encourages you to keep moving forward.

By all means, keep dreaming, and from time to time, do a reality check to make sure you're not overreaching. Ask yourself these questions:

- What is your goal?
- What will it take to reach it? (time, energy, other resources)
- Are you capable of doing that?
- If not, how can you modify your goal to make it doable? Can you give it more time? Get help? Scale it down? (See section 8, Modify and Compromise.)

When you're contemplating a new project, do a Cost/Benefit analysis to look at the benefits of doing the project and weighing it against what it will require of you. Be brutally honest with yourself up front, so that you can plan your project in a way that's achievable for you. It may require some sacrifice, but better to sacrifice a part than the whole thing.

"A pint can't hold a quart – if it holds a pint it is doing all that can be expected of it."
— Margaretta W. Deland

Worksheet 10: Goal Reality Check

Goal or project: _____

- Do I have the time to do this?

- Do I have, or can I acquire, the resources to do this?

- Do I have, or can I acquire, the skills to do this?

- What will I have to give up to do this?

- What will I have to give of myself to do this?

- Who can help me with this?

- What will I gain from doing this?

- Where will this lead me?

Worksheet II: Cost/Benefit Analysis

Goal or project: _____

List the benefits of doing this project in column 1. In column 2, list what it will cost you.

Benefits	Cost
_____	_____
_____	_____
_____	_____
_____	_____
_____	_____
_____	_____
_____	_____

Now, do the analysis:

- Do the benefits outweigh the cost?

- If not, and this is something you still want to do, how can you modify your plan to make it doable and beneficial?

- Is there an item in either column that outweighs everything in the other column? Is there a benefit that makes it all worthwhile? Is there a cost that's not worth paying no matter what the benefits?

8. Modify and Compromise

Once you've assessed the reality of your expectations, you may find you've bitten off more than you can chew. But that doesn't mean you have to give up. You may be able to modify your plan or make some compromises that would still allow you to have the "meat" or "essence" of it, without giving it up entirely.

"Compromise" carries with it a sense of losing something. Sure, it may hurt to give up big dreams, and you may need to grieve them in order to move on. But hanging on to old or impossible dreams keeps us stuck. By letting go, we free ourselves to think of ways we can attain a piece of them in smaller or different ways or move on to something we can attain completely.

Can you scale down your project or goal so that it's doable for you? Is there a different form that would satisfy your needs? For example, if you want to go into a healing profession but don't feel up to tackling medical school, is there an alternative form of healing work that would make you happy? Perhaps there is a different route that would give you the sense of fulfillment that being a doctor would. If you get satisfaction from helping people, brainstorm other ways you could do that besides physical healing work. You might, for example, teach or write about something that will help people to "heal their lives," or sell or create promotional materials for a health product you believe in.

Some Tortoises get frustrated because they can't find enough time to accomplish their projects. They feel that they need big, long chunks of time, but can't manage them, so they keep putting things off or they give up. If your project is important to you, you will need to find ways to make time for it; time just never seems to be "found."

What chores can you do more efficiently to give yourself more time for the things you want to do? Put systems in place to facilitate repetitive tasks, such as bill paying. (See section 16, Set Up Systems.) Perhaps you can string together several errands, rather than spreading them out over the week. Plan a route to minimize your distance and maximize your time.

What tasks can you delegate or hire out to make more time for yourself? One of my clients decided that it was worth paying a parking garage rather than having to move her car to the other side of the street each morning (something we do in New York City!). You might find that it's cost-effective to use a meal-delivery service rather than cooking yourself. Get your family involved, and be sure to let them know what a difference their support makes to you.

A lot can also be accomplished with small, persistent steps. How can you break your project down and strategize it, so you can fit it into the time you have? For example, plan the night before what you'd like to do the next day, rather than using up your precious time figuring it out on the fly. Find tasks you can do in a short time, such as making a phone call or looking something up on the Internet, and keep a list handy that you can refer to when you suddenly have a few free minutes. (Or you may want to use that time to rejuvenate your energy with a quick tea break or petting the dog.) (See also section 18, Break Your Goals Into Steps.)

If your dream is just too far to reach, look at the emotional gratification you hoped to get from that dream. It might be a sense of accomplishment, freedom, making a difference, working with your hands, creative expression or any number of things. This is called the "essence." Once you've pinned that down (and it may take a few tries), brainstorm ways to achieve that essence. Come up with as many ideas as you can, no matter how far-fetched or bizarre. Put the list away and pull it out later, the next day or the next week, and look at it with a fresh eye. Reread the entire list, and look for real possibilities.

Watch out for the perfectionism monster. Don't feel that you have to do everything to the highest standards or not at all. Strive for excellence, for doing your personal best. Let go of comparisons and expectations, and allow your own style and ability to shine through. Let the results surprise you, rather than feeling you have to stick to a predetermined outcome.

Be creative in finding ways to achieve the essence of your goals without getting attached to a particular form or result. Necessity is the mother of invention, and by honoring your needs and limitations, you may find yourself coming up with ideas you never would have otherwise. Like a bonsai tree, the beauty of your creations will be shaped by your limitations and enhanced by your care, attention and imagination.

"The maxim 'Nothing but perfection' may be spelled 'Paralysis.'"
— Winston Churchill

Worksheet 12: Modifying Big Dreams and Goals

Big Dream or Goal	What Part Challenges Me	Modifications I Can Make
_____	_____	_____
_____	_____	_____
_____	_____	_____
_____	_____	_____

Big Dream or Goal	Essence	Doable Alternatives
_____	_____	_____
_____	_____	_____
_____	_____	_____
_____	_____	_____

9. Keep Your Fears in Check

When our goals and dreams feel like a big stretch for us because of our Tortoise Issues, we tend to exaggerate our fears. Our creative imagination runs wild in a negative direction. We think, What will I do if my book gets published and I can't go on tour because of the kids? What if I get too tired or overwhelmed? What if I can't take the criticism? So, we don't get it published, or worse, don't even write the manuscript. We don't apply for a promotion we're capable of because we fear what will be expected of us and whether we'll be able to handle it.

Other times, we exaggerate the outcome and then fear the magnitude of our success — which may or may not happen — before we've even done anything. We hesitate to act because we don't know how we'll handle it, for example, when we get on TV in front of millions of people. Or we stop ourselves from moving into a new career because we don't yet have the skills for it; we don't even accept it as a future possibility.

While projects can take on a life of their own, you do have some control over how fast you want to move them along. I can pretty much guarantee you that if you don't go after Oprah, she won't come looking for you! If you want to make a career move, plan in advance and take steps over time to prepare yourself. If you're lacking skills or knowledge, do something about it. Don't let your fears stop you from taking the first steps. Start with step 1, and by the time you get to step 10, you'll be ready for it.

Take the power out of your fears by defining them. Think of a particular goal that scares you. Then, write out your worst fears about what might happen if you pursue it. How likely is it that that outcome will really happen? If it does, what could you do to handle it? Having a Plan B, and perhaps even Plan C and D, can take away a lot of the fear.

Do your research. Many fears are based on a lack of knowledge. It's easy to get scared when the future is nebulous. Get real, specific information on which to base your decisions, rather than speculating what might be and letting it stop you. While we can't predict the future with accuracy, it's much easier to make choices and act when you have concrete information and a well-thought-out plan to guide you.

> *"You may feel like dwelling on your limits or your fears. Don't do it . . .*
> *A perfect prescription for a squandered, unfulfilled life is to accommodate*
> *self-defeating feelings while undercutting your finest, most productive ones."*
> — Marsha Sinetar, *To Build the Life You Want, Create the Work You Love*

Worksheet 13: Alleviating Fear

Goal, project or idea _____

If I do this, the worst things that could happen are:

_____

_____

_____

Are any of these likely to happen?

_____

If yes, which one(s)?

_____

_____

_____

What could I do to prevent or handle this outcome?

_____

_____

_____

_____

What information do I need to help me move forward with more clarity and assurance?

_____

_____

_____

10. Develop Personalized Work Patterns

One of the ways we Tortoises trip ourselves up is by believing that we have to do things the way our friends and coworkers do. *Who says??* By developing your own work habits, you'll be able to get things done in a way that serves and supports your own energies and rhythms.

Here are a few strategies. A lot of these will be easier to implement if you control your own schedule. If not, incorporate what you can.

- Figure out how you work best, and schedule your day to flow with your natural rhythms. Pay attention to when you're most effective and mentally acute, when you feel alert and when you want to reach for a cup of coffee. If you're a night person or a morning person, go with it instead of fighting who you are. If your energy crashes right after lunch, include a fifteen-minute nap or meditation as part of your lunch break. You might even find a job that suits your rhythm, or find ways within your current job to accommodate your rhythms. Some industries start their day early, others late. See if your company is open to flex time or telecommuting.

  Be creative in finding ways to adjust your schedule. For example, I'm a night person, and I need time to adjust to humanity first thing in the morning. On one job, I discovered that if I brought my coffee and bagel to work and ate at my desk, my coworkers would say, "Let me know when you finish your coffee," instead of giving me work to do the minute I walked in the door. It gave me a few minutes first thing in the morning to adjust to the day and the office setting. For you, it might mean taking your lunch break, or a "coffee" break, at a time when your energy naturally slumps or closing your office door at a time of day when your energy is low or easily scattered.

- Work in spurts. Take frequent breaks to get a breath of fresh air, splash some water on your face, stretch your limbs or catch up with a phone call. Whether you're doing mental or physical work, don't expect a steady flow of energy throughout the day. You'll be more productive and creative when you don't feel run down.

> *"Imagination needs noodling – long, inefficient, happy idling, dawdling and puttering."*
> — Brenda Ueland, *If You Want to Write: A Book about Art, Independence and Spirit*

- This one is especially important if you work at home: Compartmentalize your time, so that work time is work time and personal time is personal time. By putting boundaries on when you think about work tasks and when you think about personal tasks, you'll reduce the number of things you need to hold in your mind or prioritize at any given time, thereby reducing the potential energy drain. This will also ensure that you give yourself enough time away from work, which may seem to call you 24/7. You might allot weekdays 9 to 5 (or 11 to 6, or whatever — with breaks, of course) for work, Saturdays for household and personal tasks and evenings and Sundays for leisure. Set it up whatever way works for you.

- Watch out for "dash and crash" — pushing yourself to do a lot when you feel good, and then crashing and spending the next day or two in bed. This is my "favorite," the one I still grapple with the most. I love my work, and it's hard to resist doing more when I'm feeling energetic, but I'll often find myself running on empty the next day. So, my advice is, even if you're feeling great, don't push yourself to the limit. It's important to manage your time and energy, so you don't pay for it later. At some point, put aside the work and chores and go relax and have some fun. (See tip just above.)

- Take breaks. Because we often don't feel we're accomplishing enough, we Tortoises may push ourselves mercilessly. Create resting places, like rest stops on the highway. These can be times during the day or during the week when you can catch your breath, refresh and reenergize.

  Build recovery time into your schedule. If you have a busy week, take it slow for a few days afterwards. You might set aside one weekend a month where you get away from anything that resembles work and just go play, or allot a day or two each week where you turn off the alarm and sleep as long as you want to. I find those days not only physically, but mentally and emotionally rejuvenating. Breaks are important for your physical and mental health. Don't neglect them. And paradoxically, when you do take breaks, you'll be more creative and productive.

- Find a good balance for yourself between activity and rest. The ratio may be different for you than your more-active friends. If you're energy-challenged, it's important to give yourself enough time to rest, but be careful not to use this as an excuse to not do things. Learn to distinguish between feeling tired and feeling lethargic, where inertia is dragging you down and you need to give yourself a nudge to get moving. It's easy to get into a rut, and it takes discipline to keep yourself moving at a comfortable rate. (See the section 11, Develop Positive Discipline.)

  If you do find yourself feeling lethargic, get yourself moving. Go to the gym. Take a walk while listening to some lively music, a podcast or an audiobook. Stimulate your motivation by doing something pleasurable, and allow that pleasurable feeling to carry over to the work you need to do.

- Work smart, not hard. Learn to use your energy more efficiently. Eliminate energy drains. (See section 22, Eliminate Energy Drains.) Get organized. Set up systems for repetitive tasks. (See section 16, Set Up Systems.) If necessary, get help from family and coworkers, or hire someone to take over the tasks that you can delegate, that you're least skilled at or that you dislike the most. (See section 14, Get Help.) Be willing to let go of control, that things have to be done exactly a certain way. Appreciate the help, and put the energy you're conserving toward things that will be more productive and fulfilling for you.

- Work at your own pace. It's not just about getting the work done fast. You also want to do it well, enjoy the process and feel satisfied with your performance. If you race through, you'll make mistakes and do less than your best work. Taking the time to do it right the first time will pay off in the long run. If necessary, explain to your boss that your aim is to do quality work, not just knock it out quickly.

- Use visualization techniques to help things happen more easily. Athletes often use visualization to "rehearse" their performance. You can also imagine your way through a task you need to do. Think through the best way to do it, any glitches that might occur and anticipate the most efficient order in which to do the steps that comprise it. Think of it as a chess game, where you think ahead several moves to anticipate the outcome of your next move. Thinking a project through this way can save you an inordinate amount of time and trouble.

Think of other ways to work that would be most beneficial for you and support your needs and Tortoise Issues. If you're concerned how this will be received, talk it over with family or work supervisors. Remind them of the strengths and talents you contribute, other than speed. Often, we anticipate a poor reception, when our family and coworkers want to help us do our best. They may even have a few good suggestions!

Worksheet 14: My Personalized Work Patterns

My Best Work Patterns

My most energetic time(s) of day:_____

_____

My least energetic time(s) of day:_____

_____

Scheduling Boundaries

Compartmentalize the areas of your life and the time you will devote to each.

	Day(s)	Hours
Work	_____	_____
Leisure — "me" time, family, friends, hobbies	_____	_____
Chores and errands, housekeeping	_____	_____
Other _____	_____	_____

Things I Need to Watch Out For

- ❑ Dash and crash
- ❑ Taking on too much
- ❑ Trying to rush through
- ❑ Trying to keep up with others
- ❑ Not knowing when to stop
- ❑ Not taking breaks or getting enough rest
- ❑ Not honoring my natural rhythms
- ❑ Wasting effort by not working smart
- ❑ Energy drains
- ❑ Getting lethargic
- ❑ Not thinking things through before I do them
- ❑ _____
- ❑ _____
- ❑ _____
- ❑ _____

11. Develop Positive Discipline

When I was a kid, my father forced me to practice my accordion for half an hour every day. I hated being so structured, but it set me on a path of discipline that I later refined as an adult, adding a little flexibility, and it has served me well.

As Tortoises, we will tend to approach discipline one of two ways: we will push ourselves relentlessly, or we will find any excuse to let ourselves off the hook in the name of self-care.

For those of us who push ourselves relentlessly, we need to look at the reasons why we do this. Often, the underlying cause is fear, guilt or both. Do a reality check and see if you really have something to feel fearful or guilty about. If so, work through it. When it's time to get to work, take a deep breath and release the guilt or fear, push through it or learn to coexist with it, without letting it run you.

Keep in mind that those of us in this category tend to set very high, if not impossible, standards for ourselves. We're often perfectionists. Be particularly wary of the "I'm never good enough" monster, who will tell you you're not working hard enough even if you're working every waking hour and then some. Take the "risk" of performing at less than what you consider a perfect level. Instead, strive for excellence — to the best of *your* ability. Get feedback from your managers to see how they perceive your work effort. It wouldn't surprise me if you're already performing *beyond* their expectations.

For those of us who drop to the couch at the drop of a hat, we need to develop a conscious discipline. By that I mean, disciplining yourself and developing good work habits within the limitations of your Tortoise Issue. I'm not telling you to push yourself to the point of harm, but to get yourself up and moving to the best of your ability. Your "I'm not good enough" monster may tell you you'll never get anything worthwhile accomplished anyway, so why bother. Don't listen! Remember our hero, the Tortoise, who won the race simply by taking one step after another without stopping.

Keep in mind that managing your energy is a balancing act. It will be different from day to day. Pay attention to your needs and respond to them, rather than trying to develop a catch-all plan to use in all circumstances. Develop a toolbox of strategies, refine them, choose the appropriate ones each day and make adjustments as you go.

Use the other techniques in this book to help you set and manage goals and set up systems (see sections 5 [Manage Goal Setting] and 16 [Set Up Systems]), and get human support as well to encourage you and keep you going (see section 14, Get Help). See also section 10, Develop Personalized Work Patterns.

> *"We must all suffer from one of two pains: the pain of discipline or the pain of regret. The difference is discipline weighs ounces while regret weighs tons."*
> — Jim Rohn

Worksheet 15: Positive Discipline

When I _____, I feel fearful about _____.

Is there really something to fear? If so, what can I do to lessen the fear?

When I _____, I feel guilty about _____.

Is there really something to feel guilty about? If so, what can I do about it?

Signs that I'm pushing myself too hard:

- _____
- _____
- _____

When I push myself too hard, I can stop it by:

- _____
- _____
- _____
- _____

Signs that I'm not pushing myself enough:

- _____
- _____
- _____

I can establish better discipline for myself by:

- _____
- _____
- _____
- _____

12. TAKE CARE OF YOURSELF

Taking care of yourself is a given for anybody, but as a Tortoise, it's a must, and you need to do it in a way that works for you. You may need more sleep than others. You may need a gentler form of exercise. You may be sensitive to the cold and need to dress warmer than your friends. You may need to pace your activities.

- In *The Highly Sensitive Person*, Elaine Aron talks about how, if we were treated as children in a way that was different from what we needed or desired, we continue to treat ourselves that way as adults. We may expect ourselves to endure the cold, push ourselves to the edge of our endurance or force ourselves to tolerate pain or discomfort. As an adult, you have the power to make choices that are better suited to you. If you can't take the sound volume at rock concerts or manage a five-mile hike, don't go. You can find other activities to do with your spouse or friends that aren't painful for you.

- When you're under pressure, your self-care routines, which don't have a deadline and are often repetitious and boring, may be the first to go. Don't let that happen. Like a house of cards, if you don't take care of yourself, everything else will topple.

- Have your health checked to make sure there's not a medical problem. After dragging around for several years, chalking it up to getting older, I discovered that I had a thyroid deficiency. Taking medication has not turned me into the Energizer Bunny, but I do have more, and more consistent, energy.

- Get exercise in whatever way best suits you. Find something that you enjoy that gives you the optimal level of exercise without fatiguing you. Have different types of exercise you can do when you're feeling energetic and when you're not, that are easier or more challenging. Even walking is helpful. Push yourself a little, but not to your limit. I remember hearing wellness expert Deepak Chopra, M.D., say that you shouldn't push yourself beyond 80 percent of what you could do.

  Even if you have physical limitations, there's some form and level of exercise you can handle. Find a personal trainer who will design an exercise routine just for you, or find a specialized exercise video. Collage Video (www.collagevideo.com) has DVDs for many types of exercise, including some that address special requirements.

- Get rest, when and how it best suits you. Go to bed early enough, or get up later, and/or take short naps during the day (twenty to forty-five minutes — longer ones can leave you groggy). If possible, plan your schedule around your natural rhythms, perhaps getting up late and working late, and taking a break at low-energy points. Many people find that keeping a consistent schedule, getting up and going to sleep at the same time every day, including weekends, keeps their energy more stable.

  You may also need more sleep than the average person; do your best to honor that. If you get tired during the day and need a short nap, go with it — one of my clients takes naps in her car during lunch hour. You'll be a lot more productive once you're rested, and you'll get more done than if you pushed yourself through.

> *"Sometimes I have to admit that I simply need to rest. I need to listen to my body when it tries to call a halt, and above all I need to remember that I am not so important in the scheme of things that I can't give up control (or the illusion of control) long enough to take time out."*
> — Kathleen Norris, "The Weary Woman's Manifesto," *O Magazine*

- Give yourself the best food you can. Go for the best quality. If you can afford to buy organic, do so. Choose fresh foods over packaged whenever possible. Convenience foods can save a lot of time, but make sure it's not at the expense of getting the proper nutrients. If you do use packaged foods, read the labels and look out for such red flags as sugar, salt, hydrogenated oils or anything that's on your "avoid" list. If the supermarket doesn't provide the quality you want, shop in one of the new whole foods markets that are springing up. The range of products they sell is growing every day. Avoid fast foods; most of them are just not healthy.

  Discover what foods work best for your body. Current research is finding that we're all different chemically, and different diets work best for different people. Certain foods will give you energy, while others can make you sluggish. Avail yourself of the myriad of information available in books and on the Internet (check the credibility of your sources on the latter), and do some testing to see what your body responds best to. Look out for foods you might be allergic to or have negative reactions to.

  If you're going to be out and know you won't have easy access to foods that are good for you, bring your own food with you. It's easy enough to throw something in your backpack or keep a cooler in the back seat of your car.

  Check out the vitamins and supplements on the market and see which ones might support your health and well-being. (Remember, though, that herbs are medicines that may interact with other drugs, so if you're on any prescription medications, check with your doctor before taking any.) Be discerning about what you take, as there tend to be supplement fads, and you may end up spending a lot of money on something that's not useful for you.

- Take care of yourself emotionally as well. As a Tortoise, you may have needs that your friends don't, and not understanding, they may tease you or worse. It's okay for you to stand up for yourself and set some boundaries with them. If they're not willing to respect you, you might question their value as friends. Don't force yourself to participate in events that hurt or strain you, and don't feel you need to be the brunt of anyone's jokes in order to have friends. You deserve to be treated with kindness and respect, despite your special needs.

> *"Stressed souls need the reassuring rhythm of self-nurturing rituals."*
> — Sarah Ban Breathnach, *Simple Abundance: A Daybook of Comfort and Joy*

Worksheet 16: Taking Care of Myself

Diet

Foods that are good for me:

_____   _____   _____
_____   _____   _____
_____   _____   _____

Foods that are not good for me:

_____   _____   _____
_____   _____   _____
_____   _____   _____

I need to:

- ❏ Eat more
- ❏ Eat less
- ❏ Eat more consciously
- ❏ Eat more often
- ❏ Eat less often
- ❏ Get new, healthier recipes
- ❏ Don't eat after _____ PM
- ❏ Have healthy snacks
- ❏ _____

Rest

I need to:

- ❏ Get ____ hours sleep
- ❏ Get up and go to sleep at consistent times every day
- ❏ Take naps during the day
- ❏ Take breaks
- ❏ Sleep in on weekends
- ❏ Make sure to have down time
- ❏ _____

Exercise

Types of exercise that work well for me and I enjoy:

_____   _____   _____
_____   _____   _____

Other Needs

_____   _____   _____
_____   _____   _____

13. Take Energy Breaks

Many of us push ourselves mercilessly through the day, feeling guilty about stopping even to take a breath, fearful that we won't get everything done. But energy breaks give us the fuel we need to keep going. Imagine trying to push your car to keep going when the gas tank is on "empty." It just won't go! The ten minutes you take to refuel your car allows it to go full out for many more miles.

While your body may not stop completely like a car without fuel, it will take ten times the effort to get anything done than it would if you were refreshed, and in some cases, it may leave you debilitated for a period of time. An energy break is really an investment in the rest of your day.

> *"It's hard for me not to feel guilty when my energy isn't up to the tasks at hand. But I've found it is surprisingly easy to alter my plans, to reschedule a meeting, even . . . to put off until tomorrow something I could do today. Today I would do it badly. Tomorrow, God willing, I'll be more rested and alert, and I'll be able to do it right."*
> — Kathleen Norris, "The Weary Woman's Manifesto," O Magazine

- When you find yourself getting tired or mentally foggy, stop and take a few deep breaths. Shake out your hands and even your entire body. Stretch or do some yoga, chi gong, tai chi or a few plies (knee bends) to get the energy flowing. The Gaiam catalog (www.gaiam.com) offers some beautifully done twenty-minute yoga, chi gong and Pilates tapes that are easy to fit into your day.

- Be sure to take meal breaks, to nourish and refuel your body as well, perhaps in conjunction with a walk or a leisure break. Don't skip meals; in fact, some people do better with five or six small meals rather than two or three big ones. Eat foods that are healthy for you, rather than sugar- or caffeine-loaded foods and drinks that rev you up for awhile, but cause you to crash in an hour or two. Nutrition is a very individual thing, so do some research and find out what works best for your body.

- Take a nap or meditate if you need it. It will restore and refresh mind and body, so that you can continue to work at optimal levels. You will accomplish more, and enjoy it more, when you feel good and rested.

> *"The much-maligned midday nap can be profoundly rejuvenating. Some corporations have even found that the productivity of their employees goes up when they are allowed to nap."*
> — Christiane Northrup, M.D., *The Wisdom of Menopause*

- If you're feeling burned out, make break time a priority. Take it easy for awhile. As a Tortoise, you may be particularly prone to getting sick or depleted, and you can't afford to keep pushing yourself beyond your limits. Do your best not to get to the point of burn-out, but if you do, get it handled before it gets worse. After all, if you're sick, you won't accomplish anything. Better to notch it down than lose it all.

❧ In the bigger picture, give yourself days off and take rejuvenating vacations where you're not constantly running around. While it's good, and often necessary, to be productive, you can't do it all the time. Even machines need to be refueled and oiled. And while your body and mind are much more than a machine, be sure to treat them at least as well.

Worksheet 17: Ways I Can Rejuvenate

- ❏ Take a lunch break
- ❏ Take a mid-morning break
- ❏ Take a mid-afternoon break
- ❏ Work fewer hours
- ❏ Start work earlier
- ❏ Start work later
- ❏ Exercise
- ❏ Stretch
- ❏ Take a walk
- ❏ Nap
- ❏ Meditate
- ❏ Listen to music
- ❏ Breathe
- ❏ Do something that calms and focuses me (reading, handicrafts, crossword puzzles, etc.)
- ❏ Eat something healthy
- ❏ Have a hot or cold drink (low or no sugar or caffeine)
- ❏ Sleep in on selected days
- ❏ Take time off
- ❏ Take a restful vacation
- ❏ _____
- ❏ _____
- ❏ _____
- ❏ _____
- ❏ _____
- ❏ _____
- ❏ _____
- ❏ _____
- ❏ _____
- ❏ _____

14. GET HELP

One of the "symptoms" of being a Tortoise is that our ambitions are bigger than our time and energy. One way that we can accomplish more is to "expand" ourselves by getting help.

- Find someone with compatible ambitions to partner with you. You can share ideas and the work load and accomplish a lot more than you could alone. A partner can also share the pressures and stresses of running a business, which can be an important feature for someone who's energetically challenged.

    If this is a serious, committed business partnership, take your choice of partners as seriously as you would a life partner. Make sure that your goals and ambitions are aligned, and talk about how you will proceed if things go well, if they go badly, if one person's goals change, etc. Work with a lawyer to put your decisions on paper. Like a prenup, having things worked out and in writing could save your relationship down the line, when the "honeymoon" is over and business pressures are getting to you.

    You can also partner with a friend for such things as going to the gym, sticking to a diet or making time for your creative work. Having someone who's counting on you to keep your word and show up will motivate you to do things you might slack off on your own.

- Delegate tasks to family or coworkers. Ask for their help. Often, your partner and children will be happy to help you. Offer incentives to your kids, aside from the pride they'll feel in helping you. If you're taking on too much at work, have a conversation with your manager about prioritizing your workload and perhaps handing some of it off to someone else, or you may have the authority to just redistribute work among your staff yourself. You may fear losing your job if you do less, but the people who worry about this most are usually the ones doing too much. If your manager is uncooperative, think about setting some boundaries or looking for a less stressful job.

- Hire help, particularly for the things you least like to do or are least skilled at. That way, you free up your time to do the things that will move you forward, that you do best and enjoy most and that probably earn you (or your company) more money. Contact an agency such as Merry Maids (www.merrymaids.com) for help with the housework. Have meals delivered from Family Chef (www.familychef.com), diet-to-go (diettogo.com) or Schwan's (www.schwans.com). For other tasks, find someone locally, or hire a Virtual Assistant (VA), who can do many jobs from their own space on a per-hour basis. Try some of these websites to track down a VA who's right for you:
    - www.assistu.com
    - www.ivaa.org
    - www.virtualassistants.com
    - www.virtualassistant.org

> *"Dependent people need others to get what they want. Independent people can get what they want through their own efforts. Interdependent people combine their own efforts with the efforts of others to achieve their greatest success."*
> — Stephen Covey, *The 7 Habits of Highly Effective People*

Worksheet 18: How I Can Get Help

Types of Help I Need:

Possible Sources of Help:

15. Manage Your Time

Whether your Tortoise Issue involves energy or time, it always comes down to having enough time to do everything you want and need to do. The name of the game is "efficiency." By planning ahead, you can make the most of whatever time you have.

> *"As the artists and architects of our dreams we must find ways to pace ourselves so we can go the distance."*
> — Paul & Sarah Edwards, *The Practical Dreamer's Handbook*

- One strategy I like to use is to plan a day ahead. At the end of the day, think about what you'd like to accomplish the next day. Put it in your planner, or write a to-do list for the day. You might even lay out the tools you need. You can also do this on a weekly basis, planning every Sunday for the coming week, if that works better for you. By planning ahead in this way, you can save a lot of time, as well as avoid spinning your wheels trying to figure out on the spot what to do next.

- In the spirit of matching your strategies to your personal style and needs, do your time planning in a way that works best for you. Some people are very linear and like to allot specific segments of time for specific projects. (If you do this, be careful of underestimating the amount of time a task or project will require.) Others prefer to keep a to-do list and pick things off the list when time becomes available (and your energy is up to it). This is particularly effective if your life, or your energy, is erratic and you find it hard to plan ahead.

- Be creative in developing your own strategies. Be flexible as you test them out, and feel free to make adjustments as you learn more about how you work. Be flexible, too, with the intrusions that life will inevitably thrust upon you. If your plan goes haywire for a week or two, don't throw up your hands and give up. Keep trying and making adjustments, and allow for the unexpected. Then, get back on track as soon as you can, until the next intrusion.

- Make sure you schedule the important things first. Sit down and figure out what your priorities are in life, and make sure they get some time (see section 19, Know Your Priorities). Then, fit the day-to-day chores around them. Let go of what's not important. Given the choice between taking actions that advance your dreams and priorities versus having a spotless kitchen, I'd go with the former.

- Be careful not to overschedule. Remember that things often take more time than you think they will. Set a pace that feels comfortable to you, and schedule more time than you think you'll need. If deadlines make you feel pressured, try to do without them when you can, and find other ways to motivate yourself. When I have a project in the works, I try to give myself a lot of lead time, so I don't have to get crazed trying to finish on time. If possible, I make it my goal to work on my project steadily and consistently, scheduling blocks of time in my planner and completing it whenever I can.

- When you're working on a project that's important to you, but doesn't have a deadline, set aside a block of time each day (or allot time weekly with some flexibility as to which days or hours) to make sure you keep working on it. Be realistic about how long a block of time works for you. Some people work best in short spurts, while others like the freedom of a long, uninterrupted block of time to really get into it. Sometimes, circumstances will dictate what's available.

Many of the artists I work with complain that they can't find a big enough block of time in which to focus on their creative work. Sometimes, you've got to go with what you've got. You can accomplish a lot with small, consistent blocks of time. Find tasks you can fit in when you only have a little time. The small bits of work you get done will accumulate. Work with whatever time you can scrape together, and expand it if and when you can. In the meantime, by creating momentum, you'll be able to delve into your work without a lot of preliminaries and really make the time count.

- Do give yourself a long enough block of time to push through any resistance that may come up when you sit down to work. Some of the writers and artists I work with include an extra fifteen to twenty minutes of "fussing" time at the beginning of their work period. An alternative is to create a ritual that tells your mind it's time to go to work. It may go like this: start coffeemaker, turn on computer, set out work materials, close eyes and sit quietly for two minutes, prepare coffee, get to work. Create your own.

Once again, remember that our hero, the Tortoise, won the race by being "slow and steady." You can accomplish a lot through persistence. Use planning to maximize your efforts (see section 6, Plan Ahead), and then just keep putting one foot in front of the other.

> *"To live means to experience – through doing, feeling, thinking. Experience takes place in time, so time is the ultimate scarce resource we have. Over the years, the content of experience will determine the quality of life. Therefore one of the most essential decisions any of us can make is about how one's time is allocated or invested."*
> — Mihaly Csikszentmihalyi, *Finding Flow: The Psychology of Engagement With Everyday Life*

Worksheet 19: Weekly Planner

Plan 1: Plan ahead.

- Get a day planner, either a paper one or an electronic one.
  To download a free interactive copy of my Time Management System in MS Word, go to: www.goodlifecoaching.com/TimeManagementSystem.doc.

- Fill in regular and previously scheduled appointments.

- Make a list of the projects you want to find time for, listing the specific steps you'll need to take. You may want to have a separate list of steps for each major project. (My Time Management System includes a template for this.)

- Pick the tasks you'd like to accomplish this week from the list, and schedule blocks of time during the week. (Keep in mind that tasks tend to take longer than you anticipate.) Write the tasks in your planner.

Plan 2: Choose as you go.

List 1: Make a list of your major, ongoing projects.

List 2: For each project, make a separate task list.

List 3: Make a to-do list of miscellaneous tasks that need to get done this week, including the immediate tasks from your project lists. Put important, must-do items at the top, or make them bold or highlight them.

I recommend doing these on your computer, so you can update them periodically, eliminating the completed tasks and reordering as needed, and print out clean, clear copies to work with.

Whenever you have a block of time, or even a few minutes, consult List 3 and pick something. Don't belabor what to pick. It's better to use the time to get something done rather than worrying about whether you picked the right thing.

16. Set Up Systems

One of the best ways to make the most of your time and energy is to set up systems that, once in place, will allow you to do things more quickly and efficiently. Your computer is a great tool for doing this. There are several project planning programs on the market, or you can create your own templates using word processing, spreadsheet and database programs.

A handheld PDA or smartphone, such as a Palm Pilot, iPhone or Blackberry, synchronized with your main computer, works well, too. By synching your device with your computer, you can enter your calendar and contact information once and have it on both your computer and your handheld device.

With ongoing tasks, such as paying bills and balancing your checkbook, do them on a regular schedule. For example, you might do bill paying on Thursday night and clean the house on Saturday morning. (You can do the same with repetitive tasks at work.) That way, you can write them into your planner, and they won't be forgotten.

Make use of all the incredible technology available to us. One huge timesaver for me has been doing my finances on the computer using Quicken. Not only does this automate balancing my checkbook, but when tax time comes around, it takes me a fraction of the time it used to to prepare the data for my accountant. Other software is available, including some free options on the Web. If you need something more detailed for your business, there are many small-business accounting programs, including Quickbooks, Accountedge and Peachtree.

Online bill-paying is another huge timesaver, and a great boon when you're going to be away from home. You can schedule your bills to be paid on the appropriate dates, schedule money transfers from saving accounts to checking, and then just let it go. Or you can access it on the Web from wherever you are. There's no need to handwrite a check, put it in an envelope, add a stamp and remember to mail it.

You can also put systems into place for preparing the kids' lunches, coordinating the family schedule for the week, setting up your work materials, preparing reports, grocery shopping — just about any repetitive task. It may take some effort up front, but once it's in place, it will be a huge time- and energy-saver.

See also section 22, Eliminate Energy Drains.

"Anything that is wasted effort represents wasted time. The best management of our time thus becomes linked inseparably with the best utilization of our efforts."
— Ted W. Engstrom

Worksheet 20: Systems I Can Set Up

Repetitive Tasks I Can Systemize:

- _____
- _____
- _____
- _____
- _____
- _____
- _____
- _____
- _____
- _____
- _____
- _____
- _____
- _____

How I Can Use Technology Better:

- _____
- _____
- _____
- _____
- _____
- _____
- _____
- _____
- _____
- _____
- _____
- _____
- _____
- _____

17. Do Short- and Long-Term Planning

Another aspect that overwhelms Tortoises is feeling an urgency to do it all at once. We feel that if we don't keep up with everyone else, opportunities will pass us by or something dire will happen. This is rarely true. While you may have to compromise on some dreams that you don't have the energy or motivation to pursue, you can still accomplish a lot by planning.

Break your goals down into short-term and long-term. Figure out what you can accomplish in the immediate future and what you need to allot more time for. If you're a parent, for instance, there are certain goals you may not get to, at least with any regularity, while your children are small. But that doesn't mean you have to give them up. Put them on the "back burner" and pull them out when you're ready. Or better yet, begin to take baby steps to start creating some momentum and preparing for the time when you can give it greater focus. Even if you can't yet participate in a particular activity, you can begin reading and learning about it.

You may also have goals that will take time to achieve. You may need to research options, make choices, learn new skills, develop competence and confidence or complete something else before you have the time to fit in the new goal. By planning long-term, you can begin to acquire the resources, skills or credentials you need, so that when you're ready to make your move, things will be in place. I once met a former dancer who had gone for her masters in psychology while she was still dancing. Right about the time her dancing career was coming to an end, she completed her degree and was ready to step right into a new profession: counseling dancers on dealing with career transition!

By doing short- and long-term planning, you can maximize the time you have in the immediate future and keep yourself motivated by knowing that other important dreams and goals are in the pipeline, to be picked up when you're ready.

> *"I believe you can have whatever you really want in this life, in one form or another, sooner or later. All you have to do is take care of your health and be lucky enough to live for a while. But you can't have it all at once and you can't have it forever. No life has the room for everything in it, not on the same day."*
> — Barbara Sher, *I Could Do Anything If I Only Knew What It Was*

Worksheet 21: Short- and Long-Term Goals

- List all of your major goals, both short- and long-term.

    Short-Term Goals   Long-Term Goals

    _____   _____

    _____   _____

    _____   _____

    _____   _____

- For each goal, determine the steps you'll need to take to achieve that goal. (Learn how to do this in section 18, Break Your Goals Into Steps.) For short-term goals, list the specific steps. For long-term goals, list the major components, then break the first component or two into specific steps. (Use worksheet 22, Breaking Down My Goals.) For example, if your goal is a career change and the first component is going back to school, the steps may include researching schools, getting catalogs, submitting applications, taking entrance exams, applying for financial aid, etc.

- Place your goals and steps on a time line. This may literally be a line you draw on a long sheet of butcher paper tacked on your bulletin board, or you can do it in an Excel spreadsheet, with each column representing a time segment. You might break your line down by years or in five- or ten-year segments. For goals that are complex, you may find it useful to create a separate time line that covers a shorter time period in more detail, perhaps breaking it into weeks or months.

- On the time line, place your short-term goals and the major components of your long-term goals.

- Create a one-year time line for the year ahead, broken down by months (or even weeks if that works for you). Write in the steps at the specific or approximate time you'll need to take them. Work forward a month or two at a time, or whatever feels appropriate to you, to schedule those activities. Put them in your daily planner.

Sample Time Line:

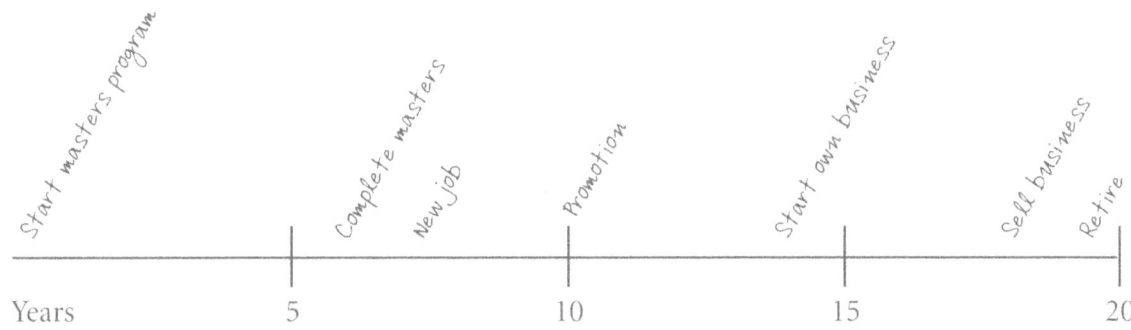

Using Excel:

	Jun	Jul	Aug	Sep	Oct	Nov	Dec	Jan	Feb	Mar	Apr	May
Get school catalogs	X											
Visit schools					X	X						
Submit applications								X				

18. Break Your Goals into Steps

Part of my definition of Tortoises is that we have big dreams. But with limited time or energy, our dreams can seem like mountains to us. To keep from getting overwhelmed and giving up, we can break our dreams and goals down into baby steps and take one at a time. You'll be surprised how far you can go this way. And when it's aligned with your natural rhythm, it'll be a lot more fun and easy.

Depending on your needs and preferences, you can do this in one of two ways:

- If you know what your goal is, work backwards to determine the steps that will get you there. Figure out the step you need to take first, and begin taking action.

- If you don't know your ultimate goal or how far you want to go with it, but do know the general direction you want to go in, figure out what the next three or four steps will be (or even one, if that's as far as you can get at this point), and start taking action. If you're not sure, pick something that seems to make sense and start doing it. If you're totally lost, start by gathering information. Once you begin, you'll see what works and what doesn't and determine your next steps. Make course corrections along the way.

For example, say you want to run the marathon. Some of the steps you need to take may include: lose weight, run every day, build stamina, improve diet. Running every day can be broken down to: buy exercise clothes and sneakers; find personal trainer, running group or partner; walk a mile every day; work up to running a mile a day; run 2 miles a day; etc.

Break your big goal down in whatever way works for you. If it gets you where you want to go in a sane, healthy way, it works! The important thing is to take one small step at a time and let that lead you to the next one. One day, you'll turn around and realize that you've come a lot farther than you ever thought you could.

> *"The 'little goal' philosophy is sagacious advice, especially for overheated enthusiasts who, tricked into believing the world is their oyster, attempt too much too fast, only to end up in defeat and frustration."*
> — Norman Vincent Peale, *Enthusiasm Makes the Difference*

Worksheet 22: Breaking Down My Goals

Big Goal or Project: _____

List the major steps you need to take to accomplish this goal. Then, number the steps in logical or chronological order.

Big Steps	Order
_____	_____
_____	_____
_____	_____
_____	_____
_____	_____
_____	_____
_____	_____

Now, take the first Big Step and break it down into smaller steps or tasks.

Big Step: _____

Small Steps	Do on or by:
_____	_____
_____	_____
_____	_____
_____	_____
_____	_____
_____	_____
_____	_____
_____	_____
_____	_____

Do this with each of the Big Steps.

Put the small steps in your planner or to-do list, and start taking action!

19. KNOW YOUR PRIORITIES

Prioritizing is difficult for a lot of people, but when your resources are limited, it's a must. As Tortoises, we may become easily overwhelmed or feel everything weighing on us at once, which drains our energy even further. By knowing your priorities, you can eliminate activities that are not serving you and approach the ones that are in an efficient and effective way.

You can do long-term prioritizing as well as short-term. (See also section 17, Do Short- and Long-Term Planning.) If you know your priorities for any given day (as well as your life priorities), you can let go of everything else or just fit it in around the important stuff, rather than draining your energy by giving everything equal weight and trying to juggle it all.

I love Stephen Covey's matrix in *The 7 Habits of Highly Effective People*. He divides activities into four quadrants based on Urgency and Importance, like this:

I Urgent Important	II Not Urgent Important
III Urgent Not Important	IV Not Urgent Not Important

Covey states that the Urgent things tend to get done, while the Important/Not Urgent ones (Quadrant II) often get lost in the shuffle. These are our long-term dreams and goals, the ones we need to make time for if we want to make them happen. By "filing" your activities into the matrix, you become aware of what your Quadrant II activities are, so you can be sure to give time to them.

A clever strategy is to move items from Quadrant II to Quadrant I by purposely making them Urgent. For example, if you want to learn public speaking, join Toastmasters and commit to giving speeches on a regular basis. If you've been procrastinating giving a class on a subject you're passionate about, commit to giving one in a specific place on a specific date. Having that commitment to someone else will make your Important item Urgent, for fear of letting someone down or embarrassing yourself by not meeting your deadline.

Once you've defined your priorities, the next step is to discipline yourself to stick to them. It's easy to allow distractions to sidetrack you or succumb to something that's nagging at you to get done, even though it's low on your priority list (like Quadrant IV busy work). If it's something you can do quickly, do it and get it over with. If not, assign it to another time or day, and let it go for now. These "little" distractions can eat up our time and energy and keep us from moving forward on our important goals. I've had writers tell me that when they have a deadline, they suddenly feel a pressing need to clean the house or wash the dishes.

> *"Sometimes we become locked into a short-term pattern of reacting to immediate needs and missing the long-term benefits of positioning ourselves to deal with more important life issues and priorities."*
> — Eric Allenbaugh, *Wake-Up Calls*

It's also important that your priorities are in synch with your values. On worksheet 5, Life/Work Values, you defined some of those values. Refer to those as you prioritize your goals. If you find an incongruence between them, it's worth considering how important those goals really are to you. Perhaps they're old, outdated goals or ones that have been imposed on you from elsewhere.

Watch out for these "shoulds." These are things we take for granted *should* be high priorities. They may be things that were important to us once and became habitual, but are no longer appropriate to who we are now. Or they may be imposed on us by the important people in our lives, the messages we get from our society and even from ourselves — the duties and obligations that capture our time and attention.

> *"You have to decide what your highest priorities are and have the courage – pleasantly, smilingly, nonapologetically – to say 'no' to other things. And the way you do that is by having a bigger 'yes' burning inside. The enemy of the 'best' is often the 'good.'"*
> — Stephen Covey, *The 7 Habits of Highly Effective People*

Bust the "shoulds" by questioning each one. Is this still important to me? Who says I should do this? Is it something I really want to do? What would happen if I didn't? Is it something I need to be responsible for (e.g., work, children)? If so, where would it fall on my priority list if I had free choice? How can I approach it in a different way or change my attitude so that I can choose it willingly?

Choose your priorities consciously, without taking anything for granted. Question each and every one of them; don't just assume its position in your priority hierarchy. Once you do that, you can allot your precious time to the things that really matter, rather than the trivia that fritters away time and energy.

> *"Know what you want to do, hold the thought firmly, and do every day what should be done, and every sunset will see you that much nearer the goal."*
> — Elbert Hubbard

Worksheet 23: Correlating Goals and Values

Make a list of your goals. Which of your values does each goal reflect? (Refer to worksheet 5, Life/Work Values.)

Goal	Related Values

Worksheet 24: Urgent vs. Important

Using Stephen Covey's matrix, classify the major and minor activities of your life. Include big things, like job, taking care of children, writing a book, getting a masters degree, as well as the day-to-day tasks, such as cleaning the house, doing laundry, responding to phone calls, taking care of yourself, dealing with e-mail, paying bills, etc.

I Urgent & Important	**II** Not Urgent & Important
III Urgent & Not Important	**IV** Not Urgent & Not Important

Matrix adapted from *The 7 Habits of Highly Effective People*, © 1989 Stephen R. Covey.

Worksheet 25: Daily Priorities

Each day, make a list of the tasks you need to accomplish. Give each task a priority number from 1 to 5, with 1 being Most Important and 5 being Least Important. If you're not sure, ask yourself, Will there be a dire consequence if this doesn't get done today? When does it *really* need to get done? Reorder your list with the 1's at the top and so on, and use it to schedule your day.

Task

Priority
1 = Most Important
5 = Least Important

Worksheet 26: Priorities: Need vs. Want

Sometimes, we give priority to the things we need to do in life, and the ones we want get lost. Use this worksheet to take inventory and provide the impetus for change.

- In column 1, list the activities you have in your life and the ones you want to introduce.
- In column 2, "Need to Do," give each item a rating from 1 to 10 based on how much you need to do it, with 10 being the highest need and 1 the lowest.
- In column 3, "Want to Do," assign a rating based on how much you want to do it, with 10 being the greatest desire and 1 the least.

Notice the items that rate high in Want and low in Need. What can you do to give them more presence in your life?

With the items that rate low in Want and high in Need, is there something you can replace them with that will satisfy the need in a more desirable way?

Activity	Need to Do	Want to Do

20. Deal Effectively with Transitions

Some of us don't do transitions well. We need time to assimilate the changes or to recover energy we expended, and we need to be gentle with ourselves. When we're railroaded through changes quickly (or railroad ourselves), it can be jarring and upsetting. Tortoises who are also Highly Sensitive (see Tortoise Issues) will probably like — or need — long transitions; it takes us a long time to get used to change.

Some transitions happen fairly quickly, while others can stretch out over a longer period of time. A transition can be simply the time between two activities, or it can be a period of change in your life, like getting used to a new job, home or relationship.

For short transitions, do your best to plan down time into your plans and activities. Actually block out time in your schedule after an activity that you expect to be overstimulating or stressful, or between two activities, to give yourself time to rest, relax and quiet your mind.

For longer transitions, begin to prepare yourself ahead, giving yourself as much lead time as you need to comfortably navigate the change. For example, if you're graduating from school and know you'll be needing to look for a job in a few months, start becoming familiar with job opportunities in your field and writing your resume.

As a Tortoise, you may need more time to adjust to new things. You may need more time to prepare in order to feel comfortable, to build confidence, to learn new skills and to just get used to the idea. Work your transitions into your long-term planning (see section 17, Do Short- and Long-Term Planning).

Of course, some transitions, such as the death of a loved one or the loss of a job, may come suddenly and unexpectedly. Even when you see it coming, such a loss is a shock. Deal with it in your own way, allowing yourself the time you need to grieve and make plans for the future. As a Tortoise, you may need more down time than you think you need. Manage the day-to-day practicalities the best you can. Don't try to go through it alone; get help and support.

Don't rush yourself through decisions. Very few things need to be acted upon immediately, and you'll feel more comfortable with your choices if you give yourself adequate time to contemplate them and feel secure in your decision. When you have something that needs to be acted on, you may feel overwhelmed and pressured to respond immediately. Instead, let it settle, think about it, feel about it and, if possible, allow a decision to emerge naturally, rather than forcing one on the spot. Most decisions are not as urgent as we think they are.

If you do need to make a quick decision, gather as much information and support as you can before choosing. Consider how trustworthy each of your sources is. Take the time to weigh the information and perhaps do a Cost/Benefit Analysis (see worksheet 11) to help you see the pros and cons more clearly.

> *"Just because we increase the speed of information doesn't mean we can increase the speed of decisions. Pondering, reflecting and ruminating are undervalued skills in our culture."*
> — Dale Dauten

You may find it useful to journal about what you're going through or discuss it with a sympathetic friend. That can help you to adjust to the changes, to process your thoughts and feelings and adapt more quickly. You may gain insights and information that will be useful in making the change.

If you're going through the transition with other people, you may find that you need more time than the others. Don't let anyone bully you into moving ahead faster than you feel capable or ready. Hold your ground and take care of your needs. This may take some practice, but when you stand up for your needs, people will learn to respect them.

We deal with transitions throughout our lives, and the more calmly and carefully you can move through them, the better you'll feel and the happier you'll be with the outcome.

". . . gradual change is usually more fruitful in the long run than is forced, ultra-aggressive upheaval. Undertaken wisely, steady transitions cultivate authenticity, groundedness, and virtues – like patience, compassion (for self and others), and perseverance. All these qualities improve your probability of success when, ultimately, you do figure out how to actualize your personal vision."
— Marsha Sinetar

Worksheet 27: Making a Decision

I need to make a decision about _____.

What I think about it:

What I feel about it:

Input I'm getting from others:
(Evaluate this carefully. Consider whether the source is someone who you trust and has your best interest in mind. Consider others' opinions, but use your own judgment.)

Pros:

Cons:

What would I choose if I had no limits or restrictions?

Is there any one factor pulling me strongly in one direction or another?

If so, what do I need to overcome if I make that choice?

21. Eliminate Distractions and Learn to Focus

Some Tortoises find it difficult to concentrate or focus. We get caught up in the activities around us and find it hard to settle down. When we're distracted, our energy gets scattered, and we don't get much done.

If distractions are your bugaboo, find ways to eliminate them. Set aside a time and a place for your activity. Close the door, turn off phone ringers, get a babysitter, close the drapes — whatever you need to do to get rid of excessive stimuli. If necessary, find a calmer place to work, such as the library or a coffee bar, someplace that takes you away from the distractions of your home or office. Or choose a different time. Some people do their best work early in the morning or late at night, when the rest of the household is asleep or the office is deserted.

If something on your mind is nagging at you, either get it done and out of the way, put it on your to-do list or set a time to do it later and let it go till then. If something catches your attention that's not relevant to what you're focusing on, drag yourself away and leave it till later. If the dramas in your life are setting your emotions afire and grabbing your attention, find ways to take your mind off them temporarily. (More on this in section 24, Manage Your Emotions.)

If focus is your issue, develop practices to strengthen focus. Set up routines that signal to you that "we're working now." Some people have to force themselves through about twenty minutes of resistance and fidgeting, until they settle down and become involved and focused. I'm told it's like a runner's high — the first twenty minutes are painful, and then it starts flowing. Think of yourself as a mental athlete, and give yourself enough time to get warmed up. Create a ritual to ease you through this time and get you set to go to work. (See worksheet 3 for some ideas on what to include in your ritual.)

Meditation and mindfulness practices can also be very useful. In life as in meditation, if you find your focus wandering, gently bring it back. Beating yourself up for losing focus or quitting in frustration doesn't help. It's more useful in the long run to develop gentle discipline. If you have a short attention span, build it as you would a muscle. Set a timer, increasing it five or fifteen minutes each day until you can concentrate as long as you want. For some people, getting up and walking around for a couple of minutes from time to time actually helps them refocus.

You can also motivate yourself to focus by setting goals. You might, for example, set a goal of writing three pages in each work session, working a certain number of hours each day or completing a project by a certain date. Treat the deadline as a game, rather than putting energy-draining pressure on yourself.

Finally, stay in the moment. Once you decide what to do in a given period of time, focus on it 100 percent, rather than worrying about whether you chose the right thing. Worry will fritter away time that could be used productively to do something — anything — from your goals list.

> *"To control attention means to control experience, and therefore the quality of life."*
> — Mihaly Csikszentmihalyi, *Finding Flow: The Psychology of Engagement with Everyday Life*

Worksheet 28: Distractions

Distractions I Need to Get Under Control or Eliminate

- ❏ Other people in the house
- ❏ Taking care of kids
- ❏ Pets
- ❏ Phone
- ❏ Internet
- ❏ E-mail
- ❏ TV / radio
- ❏ Stereo or mp3 player
- ❏ Newspaper
- ❏ Junk mail / magazines / catalogs
- ❏ Computer games
- ❏ Housework suddenly becomes compelling
- ❏ Constant "emergencies"
- ❏ Can't sit still very long
- ❏ Pursuing whatever pops into my mind
- ❏ _____
- ❏ _____
- ❏ _____
- ❏ _____
- ❏ _____
- ❏ _____
- ❏ _____
- ❏ _____
- ❏ _____
- ❏ _____
- ❏ _____
- ❏ _____
- ❏ _____
- ❏ _____
- ❏ _____
- ❏ _____

Worksheet 29: Focus

Ways I Can Strengthen My Focus

- ❏ Create a ritual or routine to start my day or work session
- ❏ Meditation practice
- ❏ Mindfulness practice
- ❏ Eliminate distractions
- ❏ Increase my attention span
- ❏ Push myself to work longer
- ❏ Push myself to read more challenging material
- ❏ Take a continuing education class at a nearby college
- ❏ Take an online class
- ❏ Work with a personal trainer to develop discipline
- ❏ Work with a personal coach to develop discipline
- ❏ _____
- ❏ _____
- ❏ _____
- ❏ _____
- ❏ _____
- ❏ _____
- ❏ _____
- ❏ _____
- ❏ _____
- ❏ _____
- ❏ _____
- ❏ _____
- ❏ _____
- ❏ _____
- ❏ _____
- ❏ _____
- ❏ _____
- ❏ _____
- ❏ _____
- ❏ _____

22. Eliminate Energy Drains

With limited energy resources, we Tortoises need to conserve the energy we have. One way we can do this is by plugging up the energy drains. In *Anatomy of the Spirit,* Caroline Myss likens our energy system to a bank account, where we receive a "deposit" of 100 energy strings a day. But if 30 strings go into worrying, another 20 to your third grade teacher who told you you'd never amount to anything, 15 to wondering whether you're doing the right thing, another 10 to the fight you're having with your boyfriend and so on, it doesn't leave you much to operate on that day. And drawing more energy than your daily allotment, like being in debt, depletes your resources and can make you ill.

In *Take Time for Your Life,* Cheryl Richardson has us uncover our energy drains in the areas of Relationships; Environment; Body, Mind and Spirit; Work; and Money. Any situation in which you feel worried, anxious, fearful, unhappy, annoyed, unappreciated, strained, uncomfortable, afraid to look at the truth or feeling you have to put on an act on a regular basis is an energy drain. It's worth your while to take a hard look at the areas of your life where you're losing energy and begin a program to "plug up the holes." This may be hard and painful work, but it will restore your energy, your time and maybe even your health.

In *There Must Be More Than This,* Judith Wright introduces the concept of "soft addictions." These are socially acceptable activities, habits and moods that we use to numb ourselves to painful emotions. They also drain our energy and squander precious time that could be used on more productive and fulfilling pursuits. Some typical soft addictions are mindlessly watching TV, surfing the Internet, overeating, overworking or feeling angry, anxious or self-pitying all the time.

Some specific Tortoise-related energy drains you can work with:

- Eliminate tasks that don't require your personal attention or that are simply busy work. Delegate, hire someone, set up a system or find a better way to do it. Handle whatever tasks are your big energy drains — the ones that feel like an unbearable burden. Hire a personal chef or house cleaner, invest in a dishwasher rather than doing them by hand or hire someone to do filing. You may feel you can't afford it, but if you investigate, you may find that it costs you less than your current strategy. Even if not, the time and stress it saves you can pay off in other ways, perhaps freeing you up to use the talents you do enjoy to make more money.

- Make sure your work space is comfortable and your equipment is in good working order. A bad desk, uncomfortable chair and poor lighting will shorten your work time and perhaps do some physical damage to you. A computer that doesn't do what you want it to do becomes a big, expensive paperweight instead of the magnificent tool it's meant to be. Invest in equipment that frees you up to do what you need to do.

- Set up systems for repetitive tasks, so you're not constantly "reinventing the wheel." This can save a tremendous amount of time and energy. Using online banking, for instance, has revolutionized my life! You can also create templates for forms you use often, organize your filing system or put recipes onto the computer, so you can find them easily and eliminate some paper clutter. (You can also use the latter strategy for organizing important papers, perhaps scanning them in.)

  Use dedicated computer programs that are set up to facilitate the tasks you need to accomplish, such as accounting and project management. I recently acquired a delightful program called SplashWallet for my Palm Pilot that keeps shopping lists and Web passwords handy and saves me a lot of time and hassle. (See also section 16, Set Up Systems.)

- Quit worrying. Worrying never did anything to ward off the evil spirits, but it does keep you from getting focused and drains your energy. Worrying is a misuse of a powerful imagination that can be used in more positive, creative ways. When I finally trained myself to stop worrying about everything, I felt like I had added another couple of hours to my day with all I was able to accomplish. It may take time, but practice taking a deep breath, releasing your worries and refocusing on the task at hand. In time, it will get easier to let go. If that's not enough, make backup Plans A, B and C, so you'll know what you can do in case the dreaded event actually does happen. That way, you can forget about it, knowing you're prepared.

- Watch out for the adrenaline rush that comes from overscheduling, being late, leaving things till the last minute and generally playing on the edge. The rush may feel exciting, and you may come to depend upon it as a motivator, but it will drain your energy, and it can become addictive. Find healthier ways to motivate yourself.

- Complete unfinished business. Anger, resentment, ungrieved losses and other unfinished business can dominate your thinking and drag you down energetically. Do what you need to do to complete these. There are many great books and audios on forgiveness and dealing with loss, as well as counselors and therapists who are trained to help you.

- Evaluate the relationships in your life. Which people make you feel happy and energized? Which ones make you feel like you were attacked by an energy vampire? The latter are toxic relationships that need to be transformed or let go. I know that's easier said than done, and may be very painful with close, intimate relationships, but they're not worth the toll they take on you, physically, mentally and emotionally. Once you work through the pain, you will feel a new freedom.

- You may also need to eliminate chemical energy drains such as sugar and caffeine. They may give you a lift for awhile, but you may find your energy is scattered and then you crash. Find natural ways to energize yourself, like doing some gentle exercise, meditating or taking a walk. If you're tired, take a nap or have a cup of herbal tea rather than pumping yourself up with a double espresso or chocolate bars.

- In general, letting go is one of the most important pieces of advice I can give you. It's easy to get caught up in running obsessive thoughts over and over again. You may choose a task from your to-do list, for instance, but then obsess about whether you made the right choice. Once you make a choice, let go of the other options, at least for the time being. Getting something — anything — done will give you one less thing to worry about and give you a sense of accomplishment.

Eliminating energy drains may seem like a major chore at first, but I guarantee you, once you begin to feel the positive effects of having your energy back, it will become easier to keep up.

> *"Every action you take uses energy. What you may not know is that actions you don't take use energy as well – mental energy, emotional energy, energy that could be used in a more positive way. . . . These things drain your energy in small ways each day."*
> — Cheryl Richardson, *Take Time for Your Life*

Worksheet 30: My Energy Drains

- ❏ Worry
- ❏ Distractions
- ❏ Obsessing
- ❏ Fear
- ❏ Anxiety
- ❏ Self-pity and related feelings
- ❏ Too many things to do
- ❏ Getting caught up in busy work
- ❏ Adrenaline rush
- ❏ Soft addictions (too much TV, mindlessly surfing the Internet, bad moods, etc.)
- ❏ Financial problems
- ❏ Relationship problems
- ❏ Unfinished business with _____
- ❏ Uncomfortable or unworkable work space
- ❏ Caffeine
- ❏ Sugar
- ❏ Other chemical addiction: _____
- ❏ _____
- ❏ _____
- ❏ _____
- ❏ _____

Changes I Can Make to Eliminate These Drains:

23. Enhance the Energy You Have

Once you've closed off the energy drains, the next step is to enhance whatever energy you have. If you're like me, your mind will initially go to popping some sort of pill. But our bodies are a natural medicine chest that we can access when we know how.

First, get excited about what you're doing. Passion and excitement are an incredible source of energy. When you love what you're doing and feel internally motivated, you become focused and absorbed in your work. You forget about your other concerns, and the time flies by. Often, you accomplish more than you expected. Some types of Tortoises, such as Highly Sensitive Persons, may still get drained easily, but your enthusiasm will give you an energy boost.

> *"Passion is energy. Feel the power that comes from focusing on what excites you."*
> — O Magazine

Similarly, Dan Baker, Ph.D. suggests in his book, *What Happy People Know*, that we can enhance our energy by focusing on our strengths rather than our weaknesses, simply because it feels better! When you live a life in which your goals, values and priorities are aligned and you're using your strengths and talents, you'll naturally feel more energized.

If you find yourself in depression or despair, handling it can restore your energy. While healing depression is beyond the scope of this book and my expertise, you can find a counselor or therapist you feel comfortable with to deal with your emotional issues, as well as coaches, workshops and self-help books to rework the parts of your life that are not working for you. While it may be scary to face your issues head-on, living with them on a daily basis is a huge energy drain. In most cases, the constant, low-grade hum of chronic anxiety is more debilitating than facing your feelings once and for all and working through them. (See also section 24, Manage Your Emotions.)

> *"Don't hold to anger, hurt or pain. They steal your energy and keep you from love."*
> — Leo Buscaglia

Find or create a positive, supportive environment. When you're surrounded by people who enjoy and encourage you, who understand your life goals, it's very energizing. You're motivated to do your best. Constant criticism, on the other hand, can undermine your self-esteem and deplete your energy. If you find yourself in this type of environment, change it or get out. As a Tortoise in particular, you may not have the stamina to endure this type of negative environment without health repercussions or selling out on yourself and your needs.

Eat right. Each of us has different body chemistry, and some of the things you're eating may be making you sluggish. Experiment by omitting your suspected troublemakers for a couple of weeks, then adding them back slowly and seeing how you feel. Experiment with the times of day you eat, as well as the size and frequency of meals. The plethora of diet books, as well as books on food allergies and nutrition, offer different ways to look at the types of foods you eat.

Lack of exercise can also make you sluggish. Like diet, exercise is a very individual thing. There are many different types and intensities of exercise, even some for people with physical limitations. Find something you enjoy, and do it at a level that feels good to you. Exercise also increases endorphins in your blood, which are natural mood enhancers. When you're in a good mood, you're bound to feel more energetic. And current research is finding that exercise is one of the best ways to keep your brain sharp and healthy.

And finally, get enough rest. You may feel you have too much to do, but being overtired is counterproductive and potentially harmful. Being rested will make you more alert and efficient, and you'll be able to accomplish more in less time. (See also section 12, Take Care of Yourself.)

Worksheet 31: Ways I Can Enhance My Energy

- ❏ Get excited about my life
- ❏ Allow myself to touch my passion
- ❏ Do things I love to do, that matter to me
- ❏ Deal with depression, despair or chronic anxiety
- ❏ Find ways to create a more supportive environment
- ❏ Eat better
- ❏ Eliminate foods I'm allergic to or that don't agree with my body chemistry
- ❏ Get more exercise
- ❏ Find an exercise regime that suits my needs
- ❏ Get more rest
- ❏ _____
- ❏ _____
- ❏ _____
- ❏ _____
- ❏ _____
- ❏ _____
- ❏ _____
- ❏ _____
- ❏ _____
- ❏ _____
- ❏ _____
- ❏ _____
- ❏ _____
- ❏ _____
- ❏ _____
- ❏ _____
- ❏ _____
- ❏ _____
- ❏ _____
- ❏ _____
- ❏ _____
- ❏ _____
- ❏ _____

24. Manage Your Emotions

For some of us Tortoises, our feelings can overwhelm and sidetrack us for a day or more. We find ourselves in a situation and obsess on the thoughts, feelings, conversations we had and what to do about it. Or we wake up one morning gripped by despair, anxiety or fear, whether for a logical reason or not, and just can't seem to shake it.

We need to find ways to work with our feelings, without denying them, so we can move forward in our lives. If you suffer from chronic depression or anxiety, or if you feel you can't do this yourself, you might want to work with a counselor or therapist to develop some strategies. Otherwise, here are a few suggestions:

- Monitor your self-talk. Very often, we take the messages that were given to us as children and continue bombarding ourselves with them as adults. We carry on the work of our tormentors. Listen to what you're saying to yourself in your head over and over again. Start writing down your self-talk. How much of it is negative? It might be a lot at first. Begin creating affirmations or mantras for yourself that contradict the negative thoughts and put them in a more positive light. Now, repeat *those* to yourself over and over again until that becomes a new habit. Continue monitoring your self-talk, and when you catch yourself in negative self-talk, replace it with your positive statements.

- Along those lines, notice the thoughts that precede your feelings. Every feeling is triggered by a thought. The process is so lightning-fast that the feelings are upon us before we even realize we've had a thought. When you find yourself in a situation where feelings are triggered, go back later and look at, What was the preceding thought that triggered that feeling? For example, say you trip and fall, and you feel embarrassed. You may have had a thought that people thought you were clumsy and awkward. In fact, they were concerned for your safety.

  As you begin to pull apart this think-feel cycle, especially for recurring emotional situations, you'll begin changing the underlying thought patterns and thus the resulting feelings. In *Feeling Good: The New Mood Therapy*, David Burns, M.D., covers in depth a number of thought patterns that can throw you into depression and how to work with them.

> *"Often we burn 70 percent of our emotional energy on what we fear might happen (90 percent of which won't happen). By devoting our energy to our other emotions, we will heal naturally."*
> Po Bronson, *What Should I Do with My Life?*

- Find constructive ways to express your feelings. Talk to a trusted friend or therapist. Keep a journal where you can safely pour out your feelings without censoring them. Write a letter to a person you're having trouble with (not to be sent!), expressing your feelings without reserve; let it all out.

- Practice speaking your truth at appropriate times, in appropriate ways. You can state your feelings in a less-threatening way using an "I" message: "When you _____, I feel _____, because _____. In the future, I would like you to _____." Note that this format does not attack the person's character or even what they did; it simply expresses how their actions made you feel. Use this general format, and adapt it to your personal style and the message you want to convey.

- When you feel upset or scattered, use a centering technique, such as meditation, prayer, yoga, tai chi or chi gong. I also find quiet music to be helpful. You might do well with exercise, a walk in nature or some spiritual practice. Create a morning ritual to start each day from a calm, centered place. Include one or more components that feel good to you and help you get centered. End the day with a calming ritual as well. (See also section 2, Calm Down and Slow Down.)

- Use focusing techniques, such as mindfulness or meditation, to refocus your mind onto something productive. (See section 21, Eliminate Distractions and Learn to Focus.) If you know that you're going to feel scattered or anxious when you work on a particular project, anticipate it by including focusing time at the beginning of your work time. Create strategies to help you release the anxiety and get focused, such as a ritual you use each time to prepare to work. Sometimes, you just have to put seat in chair and keep yourself there as you begin working, no matter how much your mind wanders, until you become absorbed in the project and get focused and the restlessness lifts.

- Some of our feelings are habitual. When we feel challenged or threatened, we may, for example, automatically fall into defensiveness or self-pity. We may wake up each morning dreading the day or feeling anxious, for no logical reason. We can treat these habitual feelings like any other habit, by replacing them with another habit that serves us better. You might diffuse a feeling of self-pity by reminding yourself that you're strong and powerful and have some control in the situation, and then contemplating what you might choose to do about it. You might even consider how someone you admire might handle such a situation. Figure out strategies to replace your unpleasant habitual feelings. Start your morning with a positive affirmation, beautiful music or time with someone you love. Keep a gratitude journal to remind yourself how fortunate you are.

- As a Tortoise, you may feel frustrated by your limitations and feel, Why bother? When we see the Hares running around us accomplishing so much, we can easily feel inadequate. But comparing yourself with others is fruitless. It can either discourage you from continuing or drive you to do more than you can handle. Accept and appreciate who you are. Keep a Success Journal to remind yourself of your accomplishments and how far you've come. Learn to appreciate your own strengths, as well as your limitations. Judge yourself on your own merits, and go for your personal best. Notice how far you've come, not just how far you still need to go. (See also section 25, Accept Yourself for Who You Are.)

- If overwhelm is your nemesis, use the techniques in this book to rework your goals and priorities so that they're manageable for you. Develop positive discipline and good work habits, and reframe the way you see yourself and your accomplishments. Work with sections 5 (Manage Goal Setting), 19 (Know Your Priorities), 11 (Develop Positive Discipline), 10 (Develop Personalized Work Patterns) and 26 (Reframe Your View).

- Finally, find an affirmation or mantra that affirms your Tortoise-ness in a positive way. For me, just remembering that the Tortoise won the race encourages me to keep taking steps, knowing that I am a winner. And while I feel like a Tortoise compared to some, there are others who think I've accomplished a lot!

> *"You can't expect to prevent negative feelings altogether. And you can't expect to experience positive feelings all the time . . . The Law of Emotional Choice directs us to acknowledge our feelings but also to refuse to get stuck in the negative ones."*
> — Greg Anderson, *The 22 Non-Negotiable Laws of Wellness*

Worksheet 32: Monitoring Self-Talk

For at least one day, monitor your self-talk. Carry around a pad, notebook or recorder, and every time you become conscious of what you're thinking, write down (or record) a few sentences, or at least the highlights.

What patterns do you notice?

Does it tend to be more negative or positive?

Is there someone earlier in your life who used to say the same things to you?

Go through and highlight all the negative statements. For each negative statement, write a positive counterpart.

Positive Self-Talk Statements

- _____
- _____
- _____
- _____
- _____
- _____
- _____
- _____
- _____

Carry the list with you, or better yet, memorize it. Continue monitoring your self-talk, and each time you catch the negative statement, deliberately replace it with its positive counterpart.

Worksheet 33: Bugaboo Emotions

The emotions I find it hardest to deal with are:

- ❏ Anxiety
- ❏ Fear
- ❏ Feeling inadequate
- ❏ Anger
- ❏ Despair
- ❏ Excitement
- ❏ Jealousy
- ❏ _____
- ❏ _____
- ❏ _____

- ❏ Depression
- ❏ Self-doubt
- ❏ Hurt
- ❏ Sadness
- ❏ Nervousness
- ❏ Happiness
- ❏ Overwhelm
- ❏ _____
- ❏ _____
- ❏ _____

The emotional situations that most often derail me are:

- ❏ Fights with my significant other
- ❏ Fights with my mother/father/siblings
- ❏ Fights with my children
- ❏ Feeling unappreciated at home or work
- ❏ Feeling inadequate
- ❏ Fear of losing my job
- ❏ Fear of losing my significant relationship(s)
- ❏ Ending a relationship
- ❏ Starting a relationship
- ❏ Feeling insecure, scared or threatened
- ❏ Feeling unable to live up to a new challenge or responsibility
- ❏ Feeling overwhelmed
- ❏ Feeling unfocused or out of balance
- ❏ Feeling out of control
- ❏ Not communicating
- ❏ Feeling trapped in a situation
- ❏ Feeling powerless
- ❏ Feeling alone or isolated
- ❏ _____
- ❏ _____
- ❏ _____

Worksheet 34: Success / Gratitude Journal

My Successes and Wins

- _____
- _____
- _____
- _____
- _____
- _____
- _____
- _____
- _____
- _____
- _____
- _____

Things I'm Grateful For

- _____
- _____
- _____
- _____
- _____
- _____
- _____
- _____
- _____
- _____
- _____
- _____

Worksheet 35: Tortoise Affirmations

- Every day in every way, I'm getting better and better.
- By taking small steps, I accomplish more every day.
- Slow and steady wins the race.
- I'm perfect just the way I am.
- By developing my unique strengths and talents, I create a fulfilling life.
- I bring value to the world in my own unique way.
- Overwhelmed today, powerful tomorrow!

Now, write some of your own:

- _____
- _____
- _____
- _____
- _____
- _____
- _____
- _____

25. Accept Yourself for Who You Are

Okay, I know this is harder than it sounds, and not just for Tortoises. Self-acceptance is a constant challenge for all of us. And, as with other aspects, being a Tortoise adds additional issues.

As a Tortoise, you may confront pressure from others to live up to *their* standards. I've been teased for carrying around a sweater during the summer because of my discomfort in heavily air-conditioned places, when everyone else was perfectly comfortable. I've felt inadequate when I've seen colleagues accomplish more and faster than I could. I've been belittled for not being able to handle what was for me a strenuous hike or for leaving a rock concert I inadvertently ended up at because I couldn't tolerate the sound level.

Ultimately, the only way to be really happy, whoever you are, is to accept yourself, quirks and all, and to take good care of your needs. We weren't put on this Earth to be clones of each other, but to be unique and express that uniqueness in our own special way. Acknowledge your strengths, and practice lovingly accepting what you see as your flaws. That may mean declining invitations to events that aren't comfortable for you — there's no valor in making yourself suffer, and you can find other activities that you can enjoy with your friends and family. It may mean calmly, but firmly asking your friends to get off your case about being different. Nobody is obligated to be the brunt of jokes or teasing.

And don't just accept, but value who you are. It's easy to diminish our innate talents and achievements, especially when they don't conform to other people's expectations, but there's no value in that, for us or anyone else. When I was working in theatre, I saw that the people who "made it" were the ones who had the courage to be who they were, in fact, to feature their differences and idiosyncracies and stand out. Use this as inspiration to change the way you look at your "flaws," to reframe them as positives. (See section 26, Reframe Your View.)

We were all made differently, with a different set of talents and qualities, so that we could contribute our uniqueness to the mix. By valuing who you are, you empower yourself to use your gifts and talents to the fullest, and that's the most loving thing you can do for yourself and most generous thing you can do for the world.

> *"If I am to stand up, help me to stand bravely.*
> *If I am to sit still, help me to sit quietly.*
> *If I am to lie low, help me to do it patiently.*
> *And if I am to do nothing, let me do it gallantly."*
> — *The Book of Common Prayer*

Worksheet 36: Accepting Myself

What I Like and Admire About Myself

- _____
- _____
- _____
- _____
- _____
- _____
- _____
- _____
- _____
- _____
- _____
- _____

Parts of Myself I Need to Love More or Learn to See Differently

- _____
- _____
- _____
- _____
- _____
- _____
- _____
- _____
- _____
- _____
- _____
- _____

26. Reframe Your View

No experience we have in life has an inherent, built-in meaning. Although it's rarely a conscious process, we interpret every event, situation and experience, giving it a particular meaning and significance. And so it is with being a Tortoise. We interpret it as being good, bad, beneficial, limiting, special, whatever. Because you endowed it with this interpretation, it's also in your power to change it.

We see and interpret life through the filters of our beliefs and attitudes. We can change our view by changing the filters. Being a Tortoise has many virtues, and while you may need to dig a little to find them, I assure you that you will.

Being a Tortoise can allow you to take the time to "smell the roses" — to enjoy the journey, not just focus on the destination. We live in a results-oriented world, and it's tempting to run from goal to goal without savoring the process. By embracing your Tortoise-hood, you can make every moment count, and not just the end result.

At one point in my career, I decided that I didn't want to set career goals for myself that were so daunting that I would hate getting out of bed in the morning. I chose to be less ambitious and instead focus on the quality of my accomplishments, rather than just the number, and to just enjoy them for what they were. It's a choice I'm happy that I made.

Being a Tortoise means listening to your inner guidance, putting your own needs first, rather than automatically jumping into the fast lane just because everyone else is there and that's the accepted thing to do. It means taking the time to make a conscious choice about where you want to put your energy. Our "limitation" forces us to find more advantageous ways to approach life.

Being a Tortoise can keep you from getting caught up in the frenetic pace of the community around you. As I get older, I become less able to tolerate driving myself to achieve. This has forced me to develop saner ways of dealing with achievement, learning to do things more efficiently, to prioritize and to let go of whatever is no longer serving me. Had I not been a Tortoise, I might have continued to push myself to the edge of my endurance and suffered the consequences. Through learning and developing positive coping strategies, life has become much more enjoyable for me.

Keep in mind that action doesn't mean achievement. We're all masters at creating busy work that gets us nowhere. I've also found that when people are asked what their greatest achievements are, they're very often the inner growth and insights they've attained, rather than the outer accomplishments. It's not about action for its own sake; it's about where it gets you. And in the work-smart-not-hard tradition, you want the actions to be as efficient as possible, producing the greatest results with the least effort.

> *"It is more important to know where you are going than to get there quickly. Do not mistake activity for achievement."*
> — Mabel Newcomber

You may also need to shift your expectations of what you can accomplish. Our world encourages us to reach for the top of the ladder, to be "the best." But you may be happier somewhere in the middle of the ladder. Rather than going for it all, you may choose to focus on one piece and do it with depth and excellence. You may want to reach the top of the ladder, but it may take longer for you than your colleagues and friends. Or you may choose to avoid the ladder altogether! Let go of the belief that you have to be in a certain place in your career or your life by a certain age, and instead, give yourself permission to follow your own path and timing.

Along those lines, you may need to let go of old dreams and ambitions. Your values and focus may have changed as you matured. A debilitating accident or illness may have left you with limited resources. You may have made different life choices than you anticipated when you set your goals; a new relationship or having a family, for example, may become more important than climbing the corporate ladder. From time to time, reevaluate your goals and dreams to see if they're still what you truly want.

> *"Another, equally important part of growing up is no longer pretending we will be able to do absolutely everything. Life is short and filled with limits and responsibilities. We each get a piece of the 'good' to enjoy, just as we each contribute a piece of that good to the world. But none of us can have it all for ourselves or do it all for others."*
> – Elaine N. Aron, *The Highly Sensitive Person*

Do what you can, and let go of what you can't. You may have to give up some of your dreams and ambitions or scale them down to where you can manage them. Choose the goals that are most important to you, and let some go or put them on the back burner. Put to rest any goals that are out of date or that you're not willing to put in the effort to achieve. Work with timing, establishing short- and long-term goals. It's better to accomplish a few things than spin your wheels trying to do it all. (See also sections 17 [Do Short- and Long-Term Planning] and 8 [Modify and Compromise].)

Take the time to figure out what's valuable about you and being a Tortoise. Look at beliefs and attitudes you hold that are limiting you or making you feel bad about yourself. (See section 25 [Accept Yourself for Who You Are].) See the bigger picture of your life, not just the immediate future. Give value to the quality of who you are and what you've accomplished, not just how much. Remember, it only takes a second or a small gesture to make a difference in someone's life.

Worksheet 37: Reframing My View

Beliefs and Attitudes

Belief or attitude: _____

Examples:
  Belief: *I have to work 12 hours a day to be successful.*
  Attitude: *If I can't write a book a year, why bother writing at all.*

Is this belief or attitude serving me?

What new belief or attitude can I adopt that serves me better?

Use this new belief or attitude as an affirmation.

Good Things About Being a Tortoise

1. It's fun to call myself a Tortoise!
2. _____
3. _____
4. _____
5. _____

Old Dreams I Need to Let Go Of

Think about a dream or goal you've had that hasn't come to fruition.

Is this something you still want to do in some form? If not, add it to this list:

- _____
- _____
- _____
- _____
- _____

Now, let go of the items on the list. Do what you need to do to get closure. You may simply need to acknowledge that you're done with it. You may need to grieve the loss. It sometimes helps to do a ritual, such as saying "good-bye" to it, having some kind of ceremony or by writing it on a piece of paper and burning it, burying it or releasing it to the wind or water.

27. Take the Time to Go Deeper

For better or worse, we live in a fast-moving world. Technology allows us to get more done in less time, but ironically, it has also elevated our expectation of *how much* we should get done. And what we lose in the process is depth. We skim over the surface of things, knowing a little about a lot, but rarely enjoying the deliciousness of plunging into a subject that we enjoy. We multitask, rather than focusing on one thing at a time. Who's got the time?!

> *"What is lost in our fast-paced society is depth. What is lost is not only the chance to reflect on our stories, but even the thought that we should want to reflect on them. In turn, what is lost is wisdom."*
> — Earnie Larsen, *Destination Joy*

If the idea of plumbing the depths intrigues you and there's something you'd like to explore, you'll need to make the time; it won't just show up. Find places where you can eliminate unnecessary tasks or do them more efficiently. Do your errands on one day, rather than scattering them through the week, and gift yourself with the "found" time to do your depth exploration. Get the busy work off your to-do list; the house doesn't have to be perfect before you can pursue your passions. Better to have a few dust bunnies and a rich life than have a gorgeous house and feel empty or frustrated because you're not exploring things you love.

Be sure to include the important people in your life here. Take the time to talk and listen to them, to spend unstructured time getting to know each other on a deeper level. One of the reasons we feel so stressed nowadays is a lack of real connection, and this is one way to remedy that. You don't need to get to know everyone intimately, but certainly those in your inner circle. Exploring people can be fascinating and satisfying.

We need to put our attention on whatever we want to grow in our lives. If you neglect the important things — and relationships — they'll wither on the vine. When you take the time to go deeper, it will feed you and calm you, and you'll be more productive with your other tasks.

Worksheet 38: Going Deeper

People I'd Like to Devote More Time To

- _____
- _____
- _____
- _____
- _____
- _____

Topics and Activities I'd Like to Explore More Deeply

- _____
- _____
- _____
- _____
- _____
- _____

Activities I Can Eliminate or Consolidate to Make More Time

- _____
- _____
- _____
- _____
- _____
- _____
- _____
- _____
- _____
- _____

28. Use the Principles of Attraction

In the interest of using energy efficiently, it's to our advantage to go with the natural flow. When you try to swim against the current, it takes much more energy to get where you're going. In the same way, when you cooperate with natural laws, things happen more easily.

One of the universal laws says that we attract what we give attention to. In our culture, we tend to focus a lot on what we don't have, what's wrong with us and what we should be. Instead, we can shift our focus to what we want to create in our lives and, at the same time, feel gratitude for what we already have. It may seem paradoxical to be grateful for what you have and, at the same time, want more, but the two go hand in hand. By feeling grateful for what you have, you're focusing on what's good, and thereby create more good.

You may feel you don't have a lot to be grateful for, especially if you're going through a challenging time, but if you stop and really think about it, you'll find many things. There is much in our culture that we take for granted, such as having plentiful food and a roof over our heads, that some people fight for every day. During the time I was writing this, we experienced a major blackout in the northeastern United States and southeastern Canada. Being without electricity and running water even for twenty-four hours made me very grateful for something I've always just expected to be there.

We also tend to create what we feel strongly about, both positive and negative. Again, train yourself to focus on the positive. Think about the new things you want in your life. Feel joy and excitement about them. When we have complete clarity about what we want, it manifests. But if you're like most people, negative thoughts will also arise — all the reasons you can't have what you want, why you don't deserve it, how you can't afford it, how you can't have it when somebody else doesn't, sadness at not having it before — the list is endless. It's like having one foot on the gas pedal and the other on the brake; the car won't move.

In order to take your foot off the brake, you need to resolve the conflicting thoughts and beliefs. One way to do this is to create positive affirmations that counteract the negative beliefs, and then burn those into your subconscious by writing them, meditating on them, posting them on the bathroom mirror or consciously repeating them to yourself whenever a negative thought comes up.

> *"There are whole books written on the subject of positive thinking and positive self-talk. . . . They truly are powerful tools for creating a life that works. I have seen incredible transformations in people . . . when they have learned how to become positive thinkers. Remember,* like attracts like. *When you are positive, you draw positive things into your life. When you are negative, you draw negative things into your life."*
> — Susan Jeffers

You can also counteract negative thoughts and beliefs by doing a reality check. Is it true that you don't deserve this success? Why not? What can you do about that? By breaking it down, you can uncover specific steps you can take to create what you want. Often, your negative beliefs were programmed into you by someone or through a bad experience. But things change, and what was true then (if it ever was true) may not be true anymore. Take the time to question your negative thoughts and beliefs, pull them apart and then do what you need to do to remedy them.

Another way to take advantage of the natural flow is to use the energy principles espoused in feng shui. Clutter blocks the flow of energy. It represents stale energy or things from the past that you're not letting go of. In order to create room for the new things you want, you need to let go of the old stuff. Take the time to clean out the closets, to get rid of things you no longer use, to go through the piles of paper and deal with them or get rid of them. You may even want to bring in a feng shui professional to optimize the flow of energy in your home or work space.

Take a look, too, at mental clutter. You may have obsessive thoughts or habitual moods that plague you. As children, we use self-pity or feeling victimized, among many other strategies, as defense mechanisms. When we're small, we often don't have the power to do otherwise. But as adults, even though we're bigger and more powerful, we continue to feel self-pity anytime things don't go our way. A feeling or mood like that can become habitual or addictive and keep us trapped in a negative, downward spiral.

Our thoughts are so much a part of us, like the air we breathe, that we tend to take them for granted. We don't realize that we have some power over them. By becoming conscious of them and replacing habitual thoughts with thoughts we choose, we can shift our outlook and change our reality. This is easier said than done, but with constant vigilance and practice, we can change those habitual thought/feeling patterns into more positive, empowering ones. (See also section 24, Manage Your Emotions.)

> *"Only one thing has to change for us to know happiness in our lives: where we focus our attention."*
> — Greg Anderson, *The 22 Non-Negotiable Laws of Wellness*

Worksheet 39: Working with Principles of Attraction

Things I Want to Create

- _____
- _____
- _____
- _____
- _____
- _____

Things I'm Grateful For

- _____
- _____
- _____
- _____
- _____
- _____

Negative Thoughts, Beliefs and Attitudes

Thought, Belief or Attitude _____

Is this true?

What can I do to change it?

What positive thought, belief or attitude can I replace it with?

29. Stay in the Present Moment

With all the technological conveniences we have, the world has become a faster place. Rather than having more time to get things done, as we anticipated back in the 1950s and '60s, everyone expects things faster. We end up feeling like we're in a race just to keep up with the day-to-day requirements and anticipate the next steps.

Most of us have a tendency to live in the past and the future. We think about what we have or haven't accomplished, and what we think we could have done better, and we plan what else we would like to accomplish. We dwell on past successes, reliving them over and over again, or dream of future successes. As Tortoises, by definition, we have big dreams, and it can become tantalizing to live in the fantasy of what we could do "if." We waste precious time and energy in fantasy, rather than using that time to do something to make it happen.

Instead, train yourself to stay "in the moment," fully focusing on and savoring what you're doing. Certainly, there's a time for planning, but if your mind is always on the future, you'll miss out on the experiences you're having. When author Susan Jeffers is having an enjoyable or meaningful experience, she makes a point of being very present for it and then reminding herself, "I have had this," so the experience doesn't just fly by without notice. Enjoy the past, but don't cling to it or live there by constantly going back to it in your thoughts and conversations.

> *"Now I understand that life can only be perfect in moments, and that we have to recognize those moments and live in them with all our heart. We need to move slowly through life, to observe and savor the present — it will never happen again — rather than dash to get to the future."*
> — Rikki Klieman, *Fairy Tales Can Come True: How a Driven Woman Changed Her Destiny*

Practice staying conscious and present. Learn meditation or mindfulness practices. Be conscious of when your mind is wandering off to the past or the future, and bring it back to what you're doing. When you're doing something unpleasant or painful, you may *want* to have your mind somewhere else, but once that becomes habit, you also drift off for the joyous and exciting moments. There's value in learning to stay present and endure the unpleasant moments. There's a saying that you can only feel the good as much as you're willing to feel the bad. The more you can feel your feelings fully, the more you'll get out of life.

30. Trust the Process

If you're like many of us, you worry about things all the time, and 99 percent of your worries never manifest. I've decided to bypass the worry and just trust that things are going to work out. So far, it's working pretty well. And in the few times when bad things do happen, I have more energy to deal with them.

Learn to listen to your inner guidance. Perhaps your Tortoise-ness reflects a life lesson you need to learn. Perhaps it's there to slow you down to appreciate all you have. Trust that your pace and path are right for you, and don't let anyone talk you out of doing what you know is right for you. You may know only in retrospect the significance of your experience. In the meantime, it may be like walking into a fog, with only your intuition to guide you toward the next step.

Practice paying attention to your intuition, so that you learn to distinguish it from the voices in your head that are not yours. Notice the results when you pay attention or not. Keep a journal of your successes. As you build a track record with working with your inner guidance, you'll begin to trust it more, and to trust yourself more.

> *"You don't have to sit on top of a mountain to discover what's right for you. You always know in your heart what you need to do. But you do have to ask yourself if you're willing to make choices. Put yourself in a position where you're making choices about your life, rather than letting other people make those choices for you. That's what balance is all about."*
> — Liz Dolan

The bottom line is, this is what you've got to work with, so make the best of it. Don't waste your energy fighting what you can't change. Practice making wise choices and taking calculated risks, so that you can maximize your potential without doing harm. Listen to your own guidance, and have the courage to march to your own drummer. The more you do it, the easier it will get, and your inner guidance will become clear and strong.

31. Learn Patience and Persistence

The final "technique" I practice is patience and persistence. In fact, it's become my personal mantra. Think of the successful writer whose first book is published only after collecting twenty-five or fifty rejections. (I actually heard of a writer who persisted through 753 rejections to get his first novel published!) Think of the actor who becomes an "overnight success" after twenty years of hard work. Your big success may be right around the corner, but if you give up, you'll never know.

My refrigerator is covered with quotes about patience. It can be frustrating to anyone when the world doesn't respond to their desires as quickly as they'd like. We Tortoises need to be especially patient with ourselves, because with our limited resources, we may not be able to put out as much effort as others do. By enjoying the steps we take, and not just focusing on reaching the goal, we can make the everyday process pleasurable. Remember, too, to be patient with and respectful of other Tortoises. You might even share your Tortoise strategies with them!

We need to be persistent as well. In coaching writers, I've discovered that you can accomplish a lot by taking small steps consistently — much better than waiting for the elusive huge blocks of time to come along and getting nothing done! Keep taking one step after the other, like our role model, the Tortoise. Keep your vision out there ahead of you as a beacon. And don't forget to take time to celebrate the small successes along the way.

> *"For a long time it had seemed to me that life was about to begin – real life. But there was always some obstacle in the way, something to be got through first, some unfinished business, time still to be served, a debt to be paid. Then life would begin. At last it dawned on me that these obstacles were my life."*
> — Fr. Alfred D'Souza

Worksheet 40: Inspiration for Patience and Persistence

- "Be patient with yourself. Self-growth is tender; it's holy ground. There's no greater investment." — Stephen Covey, *The 7 Habits of Highly Effective People*

- "To go fast, row slowly." — Norman Vincent Peale, *Positive Thinking Every Day*

- ". . . gradual change is usually more fruitful in the long run than is forced, ultra-aggressive upheaval. Undertaken wisely, steady transitions cultivate authenticity, groundedness, and virtues – like patience, compassion (for self and others), and perseverance. All these qualities improve your probability of success when, ultimately, you do figure out how to actualize your personal vision." — Marsha Sinetar, *To Build the Life You Want, Create the Work You Love*

- "When flowing water . . . meets with obstacles on its path, a blockage in its journey, it pauses. It increases in volume and strength, filling up in front of the obstacle and eventually spilling past it . . . Do not turn and run, for there is nowhere worthwhile for you to go. Do not attempt to push ahead into the danger . . . emulate the example of the water: Pause and build up your strength until the obstacle no longer represents a blockage." — from the *I Ching*

- "The butterfly becomes only when it's entirely ready." — Chinese proverb

- "Patience attains all it strives for." — St. Theresa of Avila

- "Patience and fortitude conquer all things." — Ralph Waldo Emerson

- "If you want to get somewhere you have to know where you want to go and how to get there. Then never, never, never give up." — Norman Vincent Peale, *Positive Thinking Every Day*

- "Four steps to achievement: Plan purposefully. Prepare prayerfully. Proceed positively. Pursue persistently." — William A. Ward

- "Hope begins in the dark, the stubborn hope that if you just show up and try to do the right thing, the dawn will come. You wait and watch and work: you don't give up." — Anne Lamott, *Bird by Bird: Some Instructions on Writing and Life*

- "Everyone has his superstitions. One of mine has always been when I started to go anywhere, or to do anything, never to turn back or to stop until the thing intended was accomplished." — Ulysses S. Grant

- "You can do what you want to do, accomplish what you want to accomplish, attain any reasonable objective you may have in mind . . . Not all of a sudden, perhaps not in one swift and sweeping act of achievement . . . But you can do it gradually – day by day and play by play – if you want to do it, if you will do it, if you work to do it, over a sufficiently long period of time." — William E. Holler

- "There is more to life than increasing its speed." — Mahatma Gandhi

- "You never know what agent of Providence is waiting to help if only you do your part and persist." — Judith Wright, *There Must Be More Than This*

The Tortoise View

Now that you know what your Tortoise Issues are and have some strategies in place, begin to view your world through the eyes of a Tortoise.

- See the strength and value in being who you are.
- Take things a step at a time.
- Don't push yourself faster than you can handle without damaging your physical or emotional health, your relationship, your children, etc.
- Challenge yourself to stretch and grow, but in small increments. Build the muscle before you add more weight.
- Find ways to work more efficiently. Work smarter, not harder.
- Be flexible and allow yourself to adapt to circumstances. You can be committed without being rigid.
- Listen to your inner guidance. Trust that the world isn't going to fall apart if you don't drive yourself to keep up with others.
- Find the joy in what you do accomplish and the small successes along the way.
- If you mess up or don't hit the mark, forgive yourself and try again.

Be aware that you will encounter ups and downs on your path. It won't be a straight run. When you're doing well, continue to take care of yourself; don't be tempted to push too hard. When the going is rough, do as much as you can; the good days will return. The trick is to do what you can, when you can. Use the tools and techniques in this book, along with others you discover yourself, to keep you going and keep your spirits up.

Never give up. Remember that it takes courage to be your own person and to trust that you're doing the right thing. As you work with the strategies in this book and begin to build a history of successes, your courage will grow and you will trust yourself more and more to make good choices.

If you are an Extreme Tortoise, severely challenged in one of the Tortoise Issues, and find doing any of this difficult, do what you can. Take baby steps. Doing something is better than doing nothing, and you may be surprised at what you can accomplish with small, persistent steps. Once you get some momentum going, you'll get more done in less time.

So, go forth and bring your gifts to the world . . . slowly, but surely!

"Little by little, one travels far."
— J.R.R. Tolkien

"Let's hear some good news for the lady,
She's coming out from far behind.
And if she seems a little slow,
It only goes to show
That everything will grow in its own time."

— Melissa Manchester, *Good News*

Resources

BOOKS AND AUDIOS

- *Always Looking Up: The Adventures of an Incurable Optimist* . . . Michael J. Fox
- *Anatomy of the Spirit: The Seven Stages of Power and Healing* . . . Caroline Myss
- *The Art of Extreme Self-Care: Transform Your Life One Month at a Time* . . . Cheryl Richardson
- *Balancing Act: Create an Inspiring Life Mentally, Physically and Spiritually* . . . David Essel
- *Callings: Finding and Following an Authentic Life* . . . Gregg Levoy
- *Doing Less and Having More: Five Easy Steps for Discovering What You Really Want – And Getting It* . . . Marcia Wieder
- *The Drama of the Gifted Child: The Search for the True Self* . . . Alice Miller
- *Elegant Choices, Healing Choices* . . . Marsha Sinetar
- *Embracing Your Inner Critic: Turning Self-Criticism into a Creative Asset* . . . Hal Stone, Sidra Stone
- *The Emotional Energy Factor: The Secrets High-Energy People Use to Beat Emotional Fatigue* . . . Mira Kirshenbaum
- *End the Struggle and Dance With Life: How to Build Yourself Up When the World Gets You Down* . . . Susan Jeffers, Ph.D.
- *Easier Than You Think … because life doesn't have to be so hard: The Small Changes That Add Up to a World of Difference. . .* Richard Carlson, Ph.D.
- *Feel the Fear … and Do It Anyway* . . . Susan Jeffers, Ph.D.
- *Feeling Good: The New Mood Therapy* . . . David D. Burns, M.D.
- *The 15 Second Principle: Short, Simple Steps to Achieving Long-Term Goals* . . . Al Secunda
- *Finding Flow: The Psychology of Engagement With Everyday Life* . . . Mihaly Csikszentmihalyi
- *The Gifted Adult: A Revolutionary Guide for Liberating Everyday Genius* . . . Mary-Elaine Jacobsen, Psy.D.
- *The Highly Sensitive Person: How to Thrive When the World Overwhelms You* . . . Elaine N. Aron, Ph.D.
- *How to Calm Down: Three Deep Breaths to Peace of Mind* . . . Fred L. Miller
- *In Praise of Slowness: Challenging the Cult of Speed* . . . Carl Honoré
- *Keep Going: The Art of Perseverance* . . . Joseph M. Marshall III
- *The Language of Letting Go* . . . Melody Beattie

- *Late Bloomers: 75 Remarkable People Who Found Fame, Success & Joy in the Second Half of Their Lives* . . . Brendan Gill

- *Learned Optimism: How to Change Your Mind and Your Life* . . . Martin E. P. Seligman, Ph.D.

- *Life! By Design: 6 Steps to an Extraordinary You* . . . Tom Ferry with Laura Morton

- *Life Was Never Meant to Be a Struggle* . . . Stuart Wilde

- *The Little Engine That Could* . . . Watty Piper

- *Live the Life You Love: In Ten Easy Step-by-Step Lessons* . . . Barbara Sher

- *Mind Boosters: A Guide to Natural Supplements That Enhance Your Mind, Memory, and Mood* . . . Ray Sahelian

- *Mindfulness Meditation: Cultivating the Wisdom of Your Body and Mind* . . . Jon Kabat-Zinn

- *Nothing Is Impossible: Reflections on a New Life* . . . Christopher Reeve

- *Organizing for the Creative Person* . . . Dorothy Lehmkuhl & Dolores Lamping

- *The Path of Least Resistance: Learning to Become the Creative Force in Your Own Life* . . . Robert Fritz

- *Peace Is Every Step: The Path of Mindfulness in Everyday Life* . . . Thich Nhat Hahn

- *The Power of Full Engagement: Managing Energy, Not Time, Is the Key to High Performance and Personal Renewal* . . . Jim Loehr and Tony Schwartz

- *The Power of Mindful Learning* . . . Ellen J. Langer

- *The Practical Dreamer's Handbook: Finding the Time, Money, and Energy to Live the Life You Want to Live* . . . Paul & Sarah Edwards

- *Procrastination: Why You Do It, What to Do About It Now* . . . Jane B. Burka, Ph.D. & Lenora M. Yuen, Ph.D.

- *Serenity to Go: Calming Techniques for Your Hectic Life* . . . Mina Hamilton

- *The 7 Habits of Highly Effective People* . . . Stephen Covey

- *Simplify Your Life: 100 Ways to Slow Down and Enjoy the Things That Really Matter* . . . Elaine St. James

- *Slow Down: The Fastest Way to Get Everything You Want* . . . David Essel

- *Slowing Down to the Speed of Life: How to Create a More Peaceful, Simpler Life from the Inside Out* . . . Richard Carlson and Joseph Bailey

- *Take Time for Your Life: A Personal Coach's Seven-Step Program for Creating the Life You Want* . . . Cheryl Richardson

- *There Must Be More Than This: Finding More Life, Love, and Meaning by Overcoming Your Soft Addictions* . . . Judith Wright

- *Time for Life: The Surprising Ways Americans Use Their Time* . . . John P. Robinson and Geoffrey Godbey
- *Timeshifting: Creating More Time to Enjoy Your Life* . . . Stephan Rechtschaffen, M.D.
- *The Undervalued Self: Restore Your Love/Power Balance, Transform the Inner Voice That Holds You Back, Find Your True Self-Worth* . . . Elaine N. Aron, Ph.D.
- *Unstoppable: 45 Powerful Stories of Perseverance and Triumph from People Just Like You* . . . Cynthia Kersey
- *What Happy People Know: How the New Science of Happiness Can Change Your Life for the Better* . . . Dan Baker, Ph.D. and Cameron Stauth
- *What's the Rush?: Step Out of the Race, Free Your Mind, Change Your Life* . . . James Ballard
- *Wherever You Go, There You Are: Mindfulness Meditation in Everyday Life* . . . Jon Kabat-Zinn
- *White Bears and Other Unwanted Thoughts: Suppression, Obsession, and the Psychology of Mental Control* . . . Daniel M. Wegner

OTHER RESOURCES

- Being a Tortoise in a World of Hares™
  www.beingatortoise.com

- Collage Video's Guide to Exercise Videos
  www.collagevideo.com

- Gaiam Life: Your Guide to Better Living
  www.gaiam.com

- Cheryl Richardson ~ Life Makeover Groups™
  www.cherylrichardson.com

- The Highly Sensitive Person
  www.hsperson.com

Virtual Assistants:

- www.assistu.com
- www.virtualassistants.com
- www.virtualassistant.org

Home Services:

- Merry Maids ~ www.merrymaids.com
- diet-to-go ~ www.diettogo.com
- Family Chef ~ www.familychef.com
- NetGrocer ~ www.netgrocer.com
- Schwan's ~ www.schwans.com

Index of Worksheets

1. My Tortoise Issues 10
2. My Tortoise Heroes 13
3. Morning and Evening Rituals 16
4. Setting Boundaries 18
5. Life/Work Values 20
6. Defining My Success 21
7. My Goals 23
8. Breaking Down Goals Into Steps 24
9. Project Planning 26
10. Goal Reality Check 28
11. Cost/Benefit Analysis 29
12. Modifying Big Dreams and Goals 32
13. Alleviating Fear 34
14. My Personalized Work Patterns 38
15. Positive Discipline 40
16. Taking Care of Myself 43
17. Ways I Can Rejuvenate 46
18. How I Can Get Help 48
19. Weekly Planner 51
20. Systems I Can Set Up 53
21. Long- and Short-Term Goals 55
22. Breaking Down My Goals 57
23. Correlating Goals and Values 60
24. Urgent vs. Important 61
25. Daily Priorities 62
26. Priorities: Need vs. Want 63
27. Making a Decision 66
28. Distractions 68
29. Focus 69
30. My Energy Drains 72
31. Ways I Can Enhance My Energy 75
32. Monitoring Self-Talk 78
33. Bugaboo Emotions 79
34. Success / Gratitude Journal 80
35. Tortoise Affirmations 81
36. Accepting Myself 83
37. Reframing My View 86
38. Going Deeper 88
39. Working with Principles of Attraction 91
40. Inspiration for Patience and Persistence 95

About the Author

Sharon Good, a self-proclaimed Tortoise, is President of Good Life Coaching Inc. and a Life, Career and Creativity Coach based in New York City. Sharon helps people create fulfilling lives and find work they love using the Life Purpose Process©. A graduate of Hofstra University, she is certified in Life and Career Coaching by the Life Purpose Institute and holds a certificate in Adult Career Planning and Development from New York University. Sharon coaches individuals and groups from all walks of life to create a life they love and achieve their goals. With her background in publishing, performing, photography and graphic design, she helps artists achieve their creative goals and assists writers in getting published or self-publishing their work.

As co-owner of Excalibur Publishing for 16 years, Sharon published and edited numerous books. She is the author of several books, including *Creative Marketing Tools for Coaches: Use Your Natural Gifts to Attract Your Ideal Clients*, *Managing With A Heart: 222 Ways to Make Your Employees Feel Appreciated* and *Self-Publishing Basics: Starting a Small Press and Publishing Your First Book*, as well as her e-newsletter, *Living the Creative Life*. She continues to publish her work through her new publishing company, Good Life Press (www.goodlifepress.com).

Sharon trains coaches for the Life Purpose Institute and serves as an adjunct instructor in New York University's School of Continuing and Professional Studies. She has taught workshops and teleclasses for the 92nd Street Y, Bronxville Adult School, the Learning Annex, the Career Change Network, the Virtual Reality Self-Help Center and Axxess Business Centers, among many others; has been a guest instructor at Columbia University and the Fashion Institute of Technology; and has presented for the International Coach Federation/NYC Chapter, the Independent Women's Business Circle, WorkTalk™, Friends of the Institute of Noetic Sciences and the Network of Enterprising Women.

Sharon has been featured in *Time Out NY, ARTLINE, FiLife* and the *New York Sun* and has appeared on *Life Coach TV, Coach World TV* and numerous radio shows. She is proud to be an Affiliated Coach with VocationVacations.

To learn more about Sharon and her coaching services and products, and to schedule a free introductory session, visit her websites: www.goodlifecoaching.com, www.beingatortoise.com, and www.goodlifepress.com.

www.ingramcontent.com/pod-product-compliance
Lightning Source LLC
Chambersburg PA
CBHW051213290426
44109CB00021B/2440